"Profound and powerful insight about the deepest and most important aspect of the writing process. Learning the craft of screenwriting is simply a matter of research and hard work. This book teaches you what others don't—how to access the story in your soul that will resonate with audiences."

>—Pamela Wallace, Academy Award–winning writer, *Witness, Straight From the Heart*

"An invaluable resource for writers who have mastered the basics of story-telling, but want to provide the kind of insightful creativity that enriches the story, its characters and even the writer himself!"

>—Kathie Fong Yoneda, consultant, workshop leader, author of *The Script-Selling Game*

"*The Three Wells of Screenwriting* connects you up with a long and varied world of story tellers and story tools. Follow the guidelines in this book and you'll become a more conscious—and thus more effective—media creator."

>—Pamela Jaye Smith, mythologist, international speaker-consultant, award-winning writer-producer-director, founder of MYTHWORKS

"Kalil's thoughtful and thorough book makes 'writer's block' a thing of the past. Open this book, then open your mind. You'll never be stuck on an idea again."

>—Pilar Alessandra, author of *The Coffee Break Screenwriter*

"A light and airy approach that makes screenwriting attainable."

>—Randi Richmond, senior vice-president production, UCP/NBC Universal

"I am often asked, 'How can I learn to write?' Kalil tackles this difficult question by gently reminding us that, when fearfully facing the blank page, there are multiple wells, both external and internal, from which to drink deeply when searching for something truly original and moving to say."

>—Gavin Hood, Academy Award–winning screenwriter and director, *X-men Origins: Wolverine, Eye in the Sky, Ender's Game, Rendition, Tsotsi*

"A unique and powerful aid capable of helping all types of writers. No matter what kind of writing you do, you have the 'three wells' of storytelling available to you. This book is quite simply the map and set of keys that allows you access to these three infinite sources of ideas and inspiration."

>—Forris Day Jr., host of *Rolling Tape*, commentator for *Hitch 20*

"Story comes through us. It is fluid in motion. We absorb it, we experience it, we feel it and we aspire to pass it forward. In his spiritually moving book Kalil beautifully sets up a system that guides us how to draw from three specific wells when it comes to understanding how to birth a story."

    —Jen Grisanti, story/career consultant, writing instructor at NBC, author

"Kalil plumbs the depths of the human psyche as well as what's been created to write cumulatively. He knows what makes us tick, and what makes stories durable, memorable, and resonate with all of us. Less is indeed more, and this little book proves it."

    —Dave Watson, author of *Walkabout Undone*; editor, *Movies Matter*

"A poetic look at the art of screenwriting, combined with concrete examples of how to deal with the craft."

    —David Misch, writer, *Saturday Night Live, Mork & Mindy, Police Squad!*

"*Three Wells of Screenwriting* addresses the key aspect of successful writing sorely missing in other screenplay manuals; that of the deeply personal transformative nature of writing itself, and how tapping into our deeper consciousness not only benefits our writing, but ourselves."

    —Jared Rappaport, screenwriter, professor of screenwriting, Cal State Northridge

"Kalil's breakthrough [in identifying the sources of inspiration] is defining them in clear, concrete terms—with illustrations from well-known movies—and then giving specific and engaging exercises that allow the reader to practice accessing the wells."

    —Murray Suid, screenwriter (*Summer of the Flying Saucer*), author (*Movie Quotes to Live By*)

"Can a how-to-write-scripts book be both useful and beautiful? It can, if it's Matthew Kalil's *The Three Wells of Screenwriting*. Bursting with information, history, cultural connections, practical exercises, and insights into our creative processes, Matthew's book helps us tap into the roots of our inspirations, while it inspires us to dig deeper and live and write more fully. It's a great achievement and a must-read for those who create art, and those who consume it."

    —Steve Kaplan, story consultant and author, *The Hidden Tools of Comedy* and *The Comic Hero's Journey*

The

THREE WELLS

OF SCREENWRITING

DISCOVER YOUR DEEP SOURCES OF INSPIRATION

Matthew Kalil

Foreword by Christopher Vogler, author of *The Writer's Journey*

MICHAEL WIESE PRODUCTIONS

Published by Michael Wiese Productions
12400 Ventura Blvd. #1111
Studio City, CA 91604
(818) 379-8799, (818) 986-3408 (FAX)
mw@mwp.com
www.mwp.com

Cover design by Johnny Ink. www.johnnyink.com
Copyediting by David Wright
Printed by McNaughton & Gunn

Manufactured in the United States of America

Printed on Recycled Stock

TABLE OF CONTENTS

ACKNOWLEDGMENTS

There are many people who helped get this book into the world. Firstly, a special thank you to all the writers I have been lucky enough to meet, specifically those who attended my workshops. I have learnt from each of you.

Shirley Johnston and Sjaka S. Septembir gave their detailed, expert opinions on the first vomit draft. Without you, this book wouldn't be what it is today. Dale Winton cast his eyes over early drafts. Thanks for your ongoing support.

Jurie Senekal for a lifelong friendship and for your photography talent whenever I need it.

Theresa Mallinson for a fantastic first-pass copyedit in record time. All errors left in the text are my own.

Molly Blank went above and beyond the call of duty and blessed me with a thorough edit. Molly, I am eternally grateful for your dedication and skill.

Kathie Fong Yoneda for your consistent email responses and for making introductions.

Christopher Vogler, thank you for simply telling me that I should write this book. Yours was the first book of screenwriting I read. In my journey, you are certainly a mentor figure whom I met in what felt like a very magical way. Your foreword is a final wave of your magic wand. Eternally humbled and grateful.

I was so excited the day that Michael Wiese and Ken Lee said that I would be joining the MWP family. Thank you so much for believing in this book and its message. I have learnt and taught so much from your books, and for mine to now be included among them is a dream come true. Thanks to David Wright for the final polish.

My father, Lawrence Kalil, was a great storyteller and lover of films. Thank you for starting me on this path. I know you would be proud.

To my love, Clea Mallinson. So much more than a patient reader of the first and final drafts. You helped me to focus on the main message of this book, just like you always help me to focus on my true path in life.

For my Higher Power, may you speak through this work.

FOREWORD

Some books you read, some books you live. This is one of those books you live. It is designed to be a lived experience with dimensions reaching far beyond the printed words and your thoughts as you read it. Every word of it is charged with the sense that the author has lived what he is writing about, and is trying to transmit some of that authentic feeling, in the hopes that you will be able to harness the power of your own experiences. If you trust it and begin to do the exercises and thought experiments at the ends of the chapters, you will find it is making positive changes in your writing life, and who knows, maybe in other parts of your life as well.

It will open channels to wellsprings of inspiration that you may not have known existed, or it may give you back access to sources that have been forgotten or closed off to you.

I met the author at one of those hectic, frantic screenwriting conferences that he describes in the book. He was an island of calm in that sea of excitement and high hopes, sending out a different vibration than most other people at the convention, because he seemed to be focused on something other than his own needs. He was shepherding a small group of writers who had come all the way from South Africa to Los Angeles, with aims of exposing them to the realities of the Hollywood screenwriting game and drawing attention to the great wealth of talent and story material in his native land. He had his own healthy ambitions I'm sure, but they shared space with a clear desire to be helpful and useful to others.

In a brief discussion we quickly found common ground, acknowledging the value of the mythological view of life and agreeing on the need for deeper psychological values in storytelling today. He encouraged me to find a way to visit South Africa and promised I would find a world of support there for my way of looking at stories and life, as well as some surprises.

In a short time, the opportunity to visit South Africa on business arose. South Africa was everything Matthew promised, including the surprises. I contacted Matthew and met him for dinner. Our conversation ranged far and wide, touching on our many shared interests in acting, writing, art, cooking, anthropology, animal behavior, the meaning of personal and family names, and a dozen other topics, making for a delightful evening.

At one point I mentioned an idea I formed a long time ago about how one makes a significant change in one's life, an idea involving the image of a well extending deep into the unconscious. The concept is that one has to make a clear announcement of the desire for change to all levels of one's being and all parts of one's surrounding world. The statement of intention to change, a cry from the heart, must go out in two directions: outward and inward. Outwardly, the cry must go up to the heavens, to God and the angels, and publicly to everyone around the person about to change. Inwardly, the person must figuratively shout downwards into an imaginary well that contains all parts of the personality, commanding them to get into alignment with the person's will to change. This is so that the person's intent to change will not be thwarted or confused by elements of the personality that are afraid of change or invested in things as they are, and that all parts of the person will be in agreement about the difficult adjustments that lie ahead.

As soon as I mentioned the image of the well, I noticed a slight smile on Matthew's face. He explained, "How interesting you mention wells. It so happens I am writing a book about that—about the well-springs of creativity and inspiration." I encouraged him to bring it forth as something that could be very useful for writers or anyone trying to tap into inner sources of creativity.

The resulting book makes a breakthrough in the writing craft by identifying three very different wells of inspiration and showing how they can work together to open up limitless creative potential. It flows into a wonderful, worldwide tradition that associates poetic and artistic creativity with wells, springs, fountains, waterfalls, and grottos, all of them connected by mysterious underground aquifers to boundless sources deep within the earth. The ancients believed that the earth was alive and that this interconnected web of ever-moving water was something like the nervous system of the planet, transmitting messages back and forth between us and our mother. As the author points out, the nine Muses of creative inspiration were associated with sacred wells and springs, and in one branch of Greek myth they were said to be daughters of Mnemosyne, goddess of Memory, who was also associated with a body of water, a rolling river of memory in the underworld.

This book invites you to tap into the same sources and realize the bottomless potential of your own knowledge, experiences, and intuitions, so you can make a contribution to the great river of stories that feeds the soul of the world.

Christopher Vogler
Biddeford Pool, Maine, July 2017

HOW TO USE THIS BOOK

To get the most out of this book it is best to read it cover to cover and to engage with the exercises. Learning about The Three Wells will help anyone in almost any vocation. However, the following readers may want to pay attention to certain sections.

Working Screenwriters will benefit by learning to consciously identify the wells they use every day. They should pay particular attention to chapter 8, "Acting for Writers," in order to develop their craft, and chapter 6, "Finding Your Theme," to help find stories that have to be told.

Film Professors can utilize any of the twenty-nine exercises in their classes. Teaching how to tap into The Three Wells is a deeply fulfilling experience for the teacher, as well as for the class.

First-Time Screenwriters and **Film Students** should pay particular attention to chapters 1 and 2, "Resonance" and "Experiencing The Three Wells," respectively.

Adaptation Writers should have a close look at chapter 3, "Digging the External Sources Well Deeper."

TV Writers and **Commissioned Writers** will find the idea of substitution useful, which is discussed throughout the book but especially in chapter 8, "Acting For Writers."

Those in the **rewriting** phase will find the principles presented in chapters 6 and 9, "Finding Your Theme" and "A Sense Of Place," respectively, particularly useful. Existing characters can be strengthened by utilizing the tools in chapter 7, "A Life Of Characters."

The book provides **Script Editors** with methods to help access what their writers really want to say. Chapter 6, "Finding Your Theme," and chapter 9, "A Sense Of Place," are relevant, as well as the subsection Hitting the Right Tone in chapter 10, "Live Life."

Many of the principles in this book are directly translatable for **Playwrights**, especially chapter 7, "A Life Of Characters," and chapter 8, "Acting for Writers."

Directors and **Actors** will benefit greatly through understanding their Three Wells and will find chapter 8, "Acting for Writers," particularly useful.

Even though this book uses screenwriting as a lens through which to understand The Three Wells, **Novelists, Songwriters, Journalists** and **Documentary Writers** will also profit from experiencing their wells in action by reading the chapters dedicated specifically to the wells and doing the exercises.

Finally, those with **writer's block** or **searching for their next idea** can simply do the exercises and their wellsprings of creativity will start to flow.

PREFACE

"There is no greater agony than bearing an untold story inside you."
— Maya Angelou

Today I sit at my writing desk, a steaming cup of tea beside me. Birds chirp outside my window, breaking the monotonous hum of the early-morning traffic. My laptop chimes as it boots up. I select a file that has been sitting on my desktop for more than two months. The file is a Word document called "It Must Be Written." I double-click the smooth, plastic mouse button. The file opens. I take a sip of bergamot-flavored tea as I stare at the flashing cursor. This moment enters my Memory Well and I start to type.

Even though this book is titled *The Three Wells Of Screenwriting*, I chose to name the Word document "It Must Be Written" for two reasons. Both were messages. The first was to me; the second is to you, the reader.

The first message was a reminder to myself. This manuscript, the file, shouted out at me, "must be written!" each time I switched on my computer. Writing, for me, is a chore. Or rather, getting around to it is a chore. I need a reminder. After twenty-five years of writing, an MA in screenwriting, and running workshops for almost twenty years, I knew that this book needed to be written.

It is my intention to help writers find resonance with their audiences by drawing from their distinct sources of inspiration. One way of doing this is to use our own life experiences. If I ask that of my readers, I want to ask it of myself, too. So, in this book I will share my experiences as a writer and a workshop facilitator in the hope that my readers will find resonance there. I will also share about the process of writing this book.

I suspect some readers might feel resistance to writing, as I do. I knew I wanted to write this book, but what was stopping me? Was it fear? Certainly, that was a factor. Overcoming fear is a long and drawn-out process for me, and it would take a separate book to address it. A great quote about fear is from the psychotherapist Fritz Perls, who says that, "Fear is excitement without the breath." In other words, fear and excitement come from the same place: we just have to learn how to breathe. I started to "breathe through" my fear by simply throwing words onto the screen. The words came from the gut.

I started vomiting ideas. The words tumbled onto the page. Later, I had to put on the editor's rubber gloves and dig into that vomit and rearrange the peas and bits of carrot so that they made a pretty picture. That's the rewriting process. That's where the real writing work takes place. I know a vomiting metaphor is perhaps not the best way to start a book, but if we are going to get into the depths of our writing experience, then things are going to get a bit messy. As I started this process to overcome my fear, I just needed to let the words spew forth. The strength of the vomit method is that bile comes from deep inside us . . . as do the best stories.

The second reason behind naming the file "It Must Be Written" was intended for you, the reader. I believe there are certain stories that come to us writers that must be written. You probably know what I mean. Every writer is different but, if we are lucky, a few stories will come to us from a special place.

Even though this book is about the source of our ideas, I might as well put it out there now: I don't know for sure where stories come from. There is an entire literary tradition that tries to explain the source of stories. Christians may say that the angels inspire stories. Spanish artists motivated by suffering have their Duende, a creature of the shadows. Hindus have the goddess Saraswati to inspire music, literature, and speech. The Japanese have their own version of Saraswati called Benzaiten, the "goddess of everything that flows: water, words, speech, eloquence, and music." There are many African myths that explain where stories come from, such as the Zulu story about Manzandaba, who traveled to the spirit world and returned with a sea shell that she would hold up to her ear to hear stories.

Then there are the nine Muses from classical Greek mythology. Writers would invoke the Muses when they wrote, or the Muses would write through them. What's fascinating about the Muses, particularly for this book, is that they were birthed when Zeus slept with Mnemosyne. Mnemosyne is the personification of memory.

So the Muses, who inspire our stories, are birthed from memory. This integral link between stories and memory is at the heart of many of the techniques we will explore in this book.

One common thread in various "where do stories come from" myths is that stories appear from somewhere other than the writer. It is not through a writer's own efforts or willpower alone that stories are born. Stories, some writers admit, are fragile. Nick Cave, the singer and writer, famously asked to be withdrawn from the MTV Award for Best Male Artist in 1996 because, he said, "My relationship with my muse is a delicate one at the best of times and I feel that it is my duty to protect her from influences that may offend her fragile nature. She comes to me with the gift of song and in return I treat her with the respect I feel she deserves . . ."

The more I write and the more I run writing workshops, the more I see that these old myths about the fragile muse contain a seed of truth. But the hard-bitten film industry screenwriter inside me doesn't want to believe this. It would be easier to believe that I can create stories just because I want to: it is my will alone that makes the stories come.

This belief is particularly useful for studios that want to invest in writers whom they believe can tell a story that will sell. The studios are reluctant, understandably, to invest in a "fragile muse." So we are taught to be tough, to grow a thick skin, and to kill our darling ideas. Sure, it is a tough industry and we need steely determination to survive. For years I ran writing workshops from a similar position. "Be tough and ruthless with your ideas," I would say. But, to be truly honest, when it comes to the stories that "must be written," that's not the way it works for me.

I have been lucky enough that some stories have simply come to me. I see them as golden chicks that cluster around my feet chirping for food, warmth, and attention. The more I ignore them, the louder they get, but if I don't find time to shelter and feed them, they will wither and die. Not all of these golden chicks are loud and persistent. Not all of them have to be written, but some of them, perhaps one or two, must be written.

I am not saying that we need to wait around for some "fragile muse" to strike. Far from it. If anything, I am suggesting the opposite. We could create a schedule that outlines our writing time. To get this book done I had to carve out time and write consistently from 9 a.m. to 12 p.m. each day. Just like an athlete or musician, we can train our minds and integrate structure into our creative muscles. Instead of running laps or practicing scales on a piano, if our wells of inspiration feel dry, we can use exercises like the ones in this book to dig deeper and find fresh ideas. We should aim to be tough and fit writers, but when we recognize a golden story chick we should acknowledge it and nurture it.

These are the stories that I hope this book will help you access and write. Somewhere in you, I believe, is a story that must be written. Not just told to friends and family, but written, because in the act of writing something magical and healing happens. It is my hope that we will cherish those fragile golden chicks in order to help us grow as writers and, ideally, to bring those stories into the world to make it a better place.

INTRODUCTION

*"There are three rules for writing a novel. Unfortunately,
no one knows what they are."*

— *W. Somerset Maugham*

I've seen the "how to write scripts" industry in action in Los Angeles. When attending a particular writing conference, I witnessed screenwriting gurus fighting tooth and claw for a scrap of this industry. Writers arrived eager to learn tricks that would turn their stories into blockbusters. Desperation was in the air. Screenwriters, including myself, were pitching like mad. Golden story chicks were being bartered about like livestock at a county fair. Books were being sold. Courses were being signed up for. Hopes and dreams were being dangled in front of waitresses, policemen, car-wash attendants, and teachers who write in their spare time. Do this course! Read this book! The industry seems saturated with some great, some mediocre, and some useless books on how to become the next great screenwriter. But few of those books focus on the act of writing itself. What happens in those split-second, decision-making moments when we face the flashing cursor?

This book slows down those moments. By working through the exercises you will discover that when writing we draw from three wells. The first is the External Sources Well: all the media we have consumed. The second is the Imagination Well. The third is the Memory Well. This book helps us understand and experience these wells from the writer's perspective. Then it provides systems for accessing the Three Wells so that we can make our stories fresh, original, and exciting.

I chose the metaphor of wells because the notion of a wellspring of creativity feels accurate. Wells have been with us in one form or another for centuries and have developed over time. From the simple hand-dug hole in the Kalahari Desert sand to the majestic step wells of India, such as Chand Baori, which has been featured in several movies. From the geologically complex *quantas* of Asia and North Africa, which take years to construct, to the simple bucket on the end of a pole system, known as *shadoofs* and found worldwide. All provide one of the most basic sources of life, water.

Wells have worked their way into our collective unconscious through the stories that we share. Folk tales tell of moving wells like Tobar Mhuire in Ireland that magically shifts it position over time. There are stores about cursed wells that are homes to fairies or trolls. Across the world, wells are integrated into legends told by diverse cultures. For example, in the Japanese story of Banchō Sarayashiki a woman is killed and thrown into a well only to reemerge as a haunting spirit. The Nordic myth of Mímir's Well, from which Odin drank, is a classic example of wells as sources of wisdom. Finally, we are all familiar with wishing wells. There are many around the world, such as the stunning and frequently visited well at the Qianqiu Pavilion in the Forbidden City in Beijing. Wells, it seems, hold a mysterious power over our collective imagination.

Then there are the holy wells. The Buddha is said to have magically cleared a well of grass and chaff to make the water drinkable. Wells appear in the Islamic tradition, such as the particularly evocative Hadith illustrating Allah's infinite mercy when a prostitute is forgiven because she took off her shoe and drew water out of a well to quench the thirst of a panting dog that was about to die. Wells are also often mentioned in the Bible, as in the story of Jesus meeting a woman at Jacob's well. Jesus rests alone when a Samaritan woman approaches to draw water. The fact that she was a Samaritan, had

had five husbands and was living out of wedlock meant that there was a cultural and social barrier between them. But Jesus speaks to her with no hesitation, much to the surprise of his disciples who return to find them in conversation. This story crystallizes the well as a gathering place, where cultural differences can be set aside. Communities assemble around wells, from an oasis in the deep desert to the office water cooler.

In some areas they are our lifeblood. This is wonderfully illustrated in the unforgettable well sequence from *Lawrence of Arabia* (1962) where Lawrence meets Sherif Ali for the first time. Ali shoots Lawrence's friend and guide because, "He is nothing. The well is everything!"

It's clear that wells have embedded themselves in our civilization. Their mystery, and the fact that they are the source of life-giving water, makes them a rich metaphor for where our story ideas come from.

Most screenwriting books help us analyze a story after it has been written, or before we have even started writing. We apply structure theory, character goals, desire lines, and character arcs to our scripts or to the stories still in our head. Many of these books are excellent and some are in the Suggested Reading at the back of this book. In working with these theories a lot I have noticed that they are often more useful for the rewriter, the obsessive planner, or the script editor, rather than for the writer facing the blank page in the split-second moment of creation.

Many script theorists admit that their origin is Aristotle's *Poetics*, but what came before *Poetics*? Before Aristotle's method of analysis there were decades and decades and generation upon generation of storytellers just doing what came naturally. They simply wrote or spoke from their gut. The hunters describing their hunt and the individuals who contributed to the Epic of Gilgamesh were just guys and gals sitting in front of their audiences making up stories, just as we sit in front of our laptops tapping away—sometimes tapping into something bigger than we are. We have been busy with the act of writing and storytelling for many centuries longer than we have been busy with the analysis of story structure.

This book aims to wrestle screenwriting back from the story analysts and return the power to the writer. It studies the processes at work in the moment of creation. It suggests techniques that we can put in place to help us be more authentic in those moments when we make creative decisions. Of course, it is important to have a system to help us analyze our writing. I believe, as many do, that writing, particularly scriptwriting, is rewriting. Still, it's much more rewarding to rewrite something that has elements of originality in it already because we have knowingly drawn from our wells. We can also use the wells to help us in the rewriting process, to strengthen our characters or enliven a dead scene, for example.

As you go through the book, you will find exercises at the end of certain chapters to help guide you through the process of drawing from the different wells. I find that many participants at my workshops don't like doing exercises. Even the word implies effort! However, the concepts in this book are largely experiential, so if you skip the exercises you won't get to understand them at a deep level.

There are three kinds of exercises in this book: Exercise, Exploration, and Experience. The first is simply a typical creative exercise such as thinking of a memory and then making a list. The second, Exploration, is something you will continue to do even when not reading or working with this book directly. For example, it might be watching certain movies over a period of time. Finally, we come to Experience. This is often a physical act that requires putting down the book and doing something with your body.

If you do the exercises and apply the techniques in this book you will:

1. Gain a better understanding of how resonance works in films;
2. Experience drawing from the External Sources, Imagination and Memory Wells;
3. See that all the wells are connected;
4. Learn how to consciously dig your wells deeper;
5. Discover themes and issues that are important to you;
6. Learn how to both find and develop characters; and
7. Reimagine your locations.

Many screenwriting books promise us that if we follow their instructions, our stories will sell. If we apply the techniques and exercises in this book we will, without a doubt, write more original stories and this will probably help us sell more of our work. However, this book posits that the writing process is not just about selling scripts.

Writing is about life. Writing is a journey. It's about living day-to-day and moment-to-moment as a writer. It doesn't end when we have a screenplay in production. The call to writing is a deeper and potentially more transformative one. This book taps into this transformative nature of writing through opening us up to the sources of our ideas. We will be missing one of the most rewarding aspects of writing if we don't tap into our own personal themes, fears, memories, and experiences. As Harper Lee put it: "Any writer worth his salt writes to please himself. It's a self-exploratory operation that is endless. An exorcism of not necessarily his demon, but of his divine discontent."

This book focuses on personal change through our writing, which is often more rewarding than all the little gold statuettes in the world. But, who knows, I hope it helps you collect a few of those too.

CHAPTER ONE

RESONANCE

"Language is like a cracked kettle on which we beat out tunes for bears to dance to, when all the while we long to move the stars to pity."

— *Gustav Flaubert*

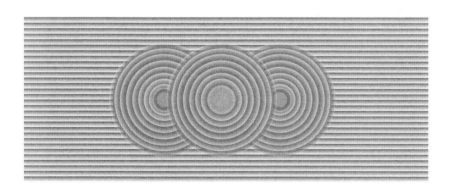

Before we look at the Three Wells of creativity, I would like to take a step back and briefly reflect on why films move us. There are many ways we can hook an audience into our films. There are plenty of books that tell us how to do so. We can use structure to make our audience care about the main character within the first ten minutes. Ensure they know the main character's goal and then make it look as if that goal is just out of reach. The audience will then probably watch until the end. We can wow them with special effects. We can make the theme so compelling that they can't tear themselves away from the screen. However, at the heart of all great forms of self-expression there is something deeper that connects the audience to the work. Again, as with the fragile muse, this process is a tricky and elusive concept to explain. I like to call it resonance.

The word *resonance* is defined in many beautiful ways and is mostly used in physics, chemistry, and music. It's a word worth looking up. I like the following two meanings: "The power to evoke enduring images, memories, and emotions," and "the reinforcement or prolongation of sound by the synchronous vibration of a neighboring object."

What happens to us when we look at a painting or an image and it moves us? Many years ago I went to the Van Gogh Museum in Amsterdam. At the time I didn't know his work very well, but as soon as I walked into the museum, the paintings immediately resonated with me. The images seemed to leap off the canvasses and into the room. They appeared to have a life of their own. I had seen reproductions but there was something about the weight of the brushstrokes and the colors that made the originals vibrate of their own accord.

I found myself transfixed before a painting called *Wheatfield with Crows*. I sat down in front of it. I can't remember how long I sat there. It was the strangest experience. This was more than twenty years ago but I can still easily recall the emotion of the moment. Time seemed to slow down. Something stirred inside me. What was it? What exactly was it that spoke to me?

That is the million-dollar question. There are many writing gurus and studios that think they know the answer. I can only talk about my experience. I felt as if I were a tuning fork and the painting was "vibrating" at a certain frequency—and that resonated with me. Something in me was deeply moved by something "moving" in the painting.

Did Van Gogh know me? Did he know how I would be feeling and plan the painting in a way that would resonate with me? Did he have me, an audience, in mind? Did he show his paintings to focus groups during different stages of their creation? Of course not. So what was Van Gogh doing when he painted?

The answer is simple, yet it's probably one of the most difficult things that we are asked to do as artists. From what I have read about his life, it seems that Van Gogh was trying to express himself and his life experience as truthfully as possible through his art. He was creating for the sake of creating. He was struggling. He was in turmoil. He was ecstatic. He was living. He was open. He was vibrating.

When I stood in front of that painting I felt that vibration. I felt that expression of self. Somehow the painting was vibrating at the same "frequency" as something in me. And so I started "vibrating." I started to "move." I was moved.

There is a great quote from the movie *Almost Famous* (2000): "All you can do is be yourself . . . and leave a pint of blood on that stage." How do we move others? We are ourselves, access our wells, and leave a pint of blood on that screen. We have to give of our lives and ourselves to truly move others. As Ernest Hemingway noted: "There is nothing to writing. All you do is sit down at a typewriter and bleed."

Now I don't mean to be all Venice Beach crystal hippie by using the word "vibration" and don't worry, this isn't one of those fuzzy, self-help writing books. We will get hands on and practical very soon. But at the heart of the craft of writing is something ethereal.

As Flaubert expressed so poetically in the quote at the top of this chapter, language often fails us when we try to get to the center of abstract things, such as why writing works. So words like "vibration" and "resonance" will have to serve.

If our task as writers who want to move an audience is to vibrate with our true selves, how do we achieve that? What can we do practically to create stories, images, dialogue, and characters that move people? That's what this book will unpack.

Van Gogh's art is raw. He sold only one painting in his lifetime, yet his images were unique and timeless—and now, priceless. It's the same with certain films. We know it when we see it because we feel it and it moves us. As Leo Tolstoy said: "Art is not a handicraft, it is the transmission of feeling the artist has experienced."

We, too, have access to those kinds of stories, characters, and images.

All we need to do is to learn how to draw from the Three Wells of creativity with confidence and serenity.

CHAPTER TWO

EXPERIENCING THE THREE WELLS

"You get ideas from daydreaming. You get ideas from being bored. You get ideas all the time. The only difference between writers and other people is we notice when we're doing it."

— *Neil Gaiman*

Let's slow down the moment of creation. Right now I have a document open on my laptop. It's a white rectangular space with a little flashing cursor. It's waiting for me to have an idea and type a letter to form a word. Before computers, we writers still faced a white rectangle: the sheet of paper in the typewriter. Before that, it was the blank page beneath the quill pen. And so on back through time.

Painters faced mostly rectangular white canvasses. Sculptors faced the white marble block. The tabula rasa in Western Philosophy is the "blank slate," or the rectangular wax tablet, awaiting inscription. In a similar way, the uncarved block of wood in Taoist philosophy, known as *Pu*, represents the ultimate art form because it can become anything. In its uncarved state it contains unlimited possibilities.

I like to think of the rectangular history of my laptop screen going all the way back to the tabula rasa. It reminds me that we face infinity each time we start to create. We stare at the blank page and we can write anything. We face countless choices regarding characters, dialogue, scenes, and actions.

So what exactly happens when I face infinity on my page? If I pause at that moment just before I start typing, I can feel my mind going to one of three distinct sources, or wells, from which to draw my story ideas. These three wells are connected and seep into one another, but I can consciously identify which one I am drawing from as I create.

The Three Wells are:
1. The External Sources Well;
2. The Imagination Well; and
3. The Memory Well.

These wells are universal. They apply to anyone, anywhere. Anybody trying to do something creative will tap into these wells whether they know it or not. The wells apply to all people in the arts be they architects, musicians, painters, actors, or dancers. They also apply to everyone in the filmmaking process and to people in business who want to leap beyond the traditional structures of their field and make creative decisions. It may seem like a stretch but the wells even apply to the sportsperson on the field, trying to make a creative play.

THE EXTERNAL SOURCES WELL

When it comes to screenwriting, this well is filled with all the movies we've seen and books we've read. It is our mind's cache of media such as TV series, YouTube clips, and Facebook posts. It is more of a reservoir with a tap on the end than a well. Someone else has collected the water and there is a tap to release it. All we have to do is open the tap and out it flows.

To fully understand this concept, it is important that you do the exercises in this chapter. There is no right or wrong way of doing them. They are there to let us experience what it feels like to tap into these different sources within us.

Turn to the end of this chapter and do the Graveyard Exercise where you will pretend that you have to write a funeral scene.

It is highly recommended that you do the exercise before reading further.

The immediate things I think of when first doing this exercise are:
- Granite headstones
- Green, well-trimmed grass

- Oak trees
- Statues of angels
- Rain
- Umbrellas
- Damp, dark soil
- Grieving widow behind black veil
- Priest in robes with small Bible
- Mourners in smart, black clothing
- A row of small chairs
- Someone watching at a distance, excluded

We may have activated our imagination or memory during this exercise, but often the first well we draw from is the External Sources Well. There is nothing inherently wrong with drawing from this well, but it can result in cliché. We've all seen the images mentioned above in funeral scenes. The films we watch colonize our mind. Sure, we could create an entirely entertaining movie from the External Sources Well. Superhero movies and action films all draw heavily from this well, but some don't necessarily resonate with us as deeply as they could.

The External Sources Well also includes non-film sources such as newspaper articles, biographies, histories, or stories that we have read or heard. These are other people's stories, or rather, strangers' stories. We can access them, but they are not our experiences. We may be able to imagine ourselves into a stranger's shoes, but if we have never met them, or been to the places they live in, then this is still an external experience.

If we do extensive background research around these secondary sources, we can gain context and then shift the focus deeper into the Memory Well, which we will look at later. But for now, don't forget that this kind of secondary research material also falls under the External Sources Well.

For most writers the External Sources Well is a safe, easy, and instant well to draw from. It's the path of least resistance. It has its advantages, especially when we are writing to a deadline. Films drawn from this well often make the viewer feel safe. We can watch episode after episode of a superhero TV series and it feels comfortable, like putting on a worn jacket. We know what to expect. We aren't challenged and can eat our popcorn and, if we like, fall asleep.

Drawing from this well does not guarantee deep resonance with our audiences. If we want to write something that will resonate and is true to ourselves, we shouldn't draw from this well alone.

THE IMAGINATION WELL

If I consciously tell my mind not to draw from the External Sources Well, I have two other wells I can access. My mind splits between the Imagination Well and the Memory Well. Some people find getting into their Memory Well easier than their Imagination Well. For me, my mind goes to the Imagination Well next.

Imagination is a tricky concept and the myths surrounding it are often about "divine inspiration." It's the flash of lightning from above. The External Sources Well is the path of least resistance. It's easy to access. It can be almost instantaneous. The Imagination Well requires that we pause for a nanosecond before accessing it. It's that moment when the writer puts pen into mouth and looks heavenward, waiting and then . . . bam, an idea arrives as if from Zeus's lightning bolt and he or she leaps into ecstatic writing.

Great flights of fantasy can happen with this well. Anything is possible.

To feel the Imagination Well in action, turn to the end of this chapter and do the Imagined Graveyard Exercise where you will make up a graveyard scene.

Did you feel what it felt like to draw from this well? Did it feel distinct from the External Sources Well?

With this exercise, if I just let my mind go wild, I think of:

- A burial in space
- The congregation all on hoverboards
- The corpse rises from the coffin
- It starts raining snails
- All the mourners are wearing clown noses

Drawing from this well is fun. It feels creative. It's what many non-writers think that writing is all about. It's often described as "fueling the imagination" or "freeing the imagination." It can be playful. Kids tap into it with ease, making up hours of stories while they play. Unfortunately, for a lot of people, growing up includes sealing off this well. I will talk later about how to re-access it.

Many fantastic films come from this well. A lot of Steven Spielberg's films are drawn from here. His writers also seem to tap into their Memory Wells, as seen in observed moments such as the family dinner-table scenes in *Close Encounters of the Third Kind* (1977). It's a potent combination of wells.

Entire genres, such as sci-fi and fantasy, are inspired by, and devoted to, the Imagination Well alone. The plethora of fantasy novels is proof that this well results in an explosion of ideas. It never seems to dry up. As with all the wells though, this one also has a weakness.

One of the issues with drawing from imagination and fantasy only is that the resulting stories are often not rooted in reality. I see it time and again at my writing workshops. The participants tap into a combination of the External Sources and Imagination Wells and come up with far-fetched ideas. For some reason, many of them like to create stories about prostitutes, homeless people, or drug addicts, which often don't ring true.

The first script I wrote was about a homeless woman. I tried to put myself in the shoes of someone who lived on the slopes of a mountain and walked down to the main road to scavenge in dustbins. I imagined a story of how she had come to this point. I fantasized about her rural upbringing with little money. She had to leave home. She hitched to the big town and lived with her uncle, who abused her. She worked in a textile factory but lost her job and ended up in the streets. I imagined the entire story. But the final script didn't resonate.

Why didn't it work? It was structured well enough. It had some evocative images and great moments. But something was missing. It didn't ring true. It wasn't rooted in reality. Sure, it could have been an entertaining story, but I didn't know her story. I hadn't done any thorough research. I had only tapped into my Imagination Well, and as a result the script lacked authenticity.

THE MEMORY WELL

This is the final well that my mind goes to when facing the flashing cursor. It's the most difficult to access, but contains the freshest water. It is filled with our personal memories and experiences: People we've met, exchanges and experiences we've had, places we've been to, and complex emotions we've felt. It is the sum total of our life experience. It contains a depth we can hardly imagine.

This well is raw and real. It's connected to us personally. For many writers this well is terrifying. There are many reasons for this, but one is that when we look into this well we may see ourselves reflected back, and we may not like what we see.

Tapping into the Memory Well means feeling emotions. When I access the External Sources or Imagination Wells, all I feel are escapist emotions. Elation, freedom, and amusement are some of the easy feelings we encounter when creating that way. These emotions are relatively undemanding to experience. Grappling with our memories—especially if many of us have learnt to close them off from a very young age—is much more difficult. These emotions may make us feel vulnerable.

Many of us have boarded up this rich, creative well. But if we are willing to go there, to work through and with our memories, we can tap into some really powerful emotions. If we are brave enough to explore this well we will feel, and if we can express those feelings, we are more likely to write something that will resonate with our audiences. This is brave writing and not for the fainthearted.

In a moment you will turn to the end of this chapter and do the Graveyard from Life Exercise. But before you do that, a few more words about drawing from the Memory Well.

It takes a nanosecond, or a moment of pause, to access the Imagination Well, but it takes an even longer and deeper pause to access the Memory Well. We have to sit with it, sift through our lives, and recall experiences we've had. We need to reflect.

This can be emotionally challenging; it might be traumatic if we push ourselves to recall the death of a loved one, for example. Or, perhaps we reflect on a funeral we attended when we didn't really want to be there. We might find shame there. Accessing memories can be difficult or easy, depending on the memory and how emotional or sensitive we are in our day-to-day lives.

William Wordsworth said: "Poetry is the spontaneous overflow of powerful feelings: it takes its origin from emotion recollected in tranquility." There are two ideas I would like to look at here. The first is that he doesn't use the word memory, but rather emotion. Recalling memories is more about recalling an emotional experience than an actual event. In the Graveyard from Life Exercise, you will be asked to recall a precise moment in time. It might seem simple, as if I'm just asking you to remember an event. But many people in my workshops get stuck, because they feel they have to recall the memory perfectly. They think they have to "get the order of events right."

Memory, however, is not only about events, but also about experiences and emotion. This is an important distinction, because it alleviates any concern about remembering events precisely as they happened. Each person remembers the same event in slightly different ways because we mediate it through our senses. It's impossible for us to see the world objectively, and so it's impossible for us to recall events objectively. When we store a memory, we are storing our subjective experience of an event, and it's that experience that has power. It's that experience we have to tap into to transmit a similar experience to our audience. It is an "emotion" recalled, not an event.

A second idea from the Wordsworth quote worth looking at is that he uses the word "tranquility." When accessing the Memory

Well, tranquility is needed. This is the longer and deeper pause I referred to earlier.

For Wordsworth, and for many writers, making space in their lives for tranquility was not just about finding the time to write, but about opening up the space for deep recollection of emotions and memories. When you do the exercises in this book relating to memory, feel what this moment of stillness feels like. Learn to know, appreciate, and cultivate it.

Enough theory about the process: I want us to feel it in action. Turn to the end of this chapter and do the Graveyard from Life Exercise. We must not be afraid to go deep. Take a long moment. Take as long as you need to find some tranquility. Savor the memories.

If you still haven't done the exercise, then turn to the end of this chapter and do it. Close the book if you have to. Put it away. Spend some time recalling your past.

Here are some things that come to my mind when I reflect on two graveyards I have been to:

Graveyard in a desert:
- Hard, semi-desert earth
- Almost impossible to dig into
- Red sand
- Hot sun
- Plastic flowers, stuck into Coke bottles
- Wind

Graveyard in an orange orchard:
- Broken wire fence
- Orange blossoms floating through the scene
- Tiny wooden crosses

- Broken bits of colored glass stuck into shapes to make unique headstones
- A citrus smell
- Soft mounds of freshly tilled soil

When they first try this exercise, many of my workshop participants immediately say they haven't seen enough graveyards. But once they put their minds to it and dig in a bit, they often come back with the most remarkable images or stories. It's not easy. Some struggle. You might also have struggled. But once they start sharing their unique events the energy in the room shifts. It becomes charged with true life experiences. Some participants laugh, cry, and are moved. They connect. The air feels as if it's vibrating with fresh stories and ideas. This is how we achieve resonance.

We might think that by using our Imagination Well we have invented a graveyard scene no one has seen before. Maybe we did, but here, in the Memory Well, the scenes we create from our recollections and memories become specific and unique. They become fresh and individual.

I wrote my second short script just after I wrote my first one about the homeless woman. This time I drew from my memories. It's called *The Sergeant Major's Dream* and is based on my experiences in the army. It's the story about a young cadet who is under the heel of an abusive sergeant major and decides, in his powerlessness, to curse the sergeant major using a made-up ritual. Through a series of events the young cadet obtains a cigarette smoked by the sergeant major and, through what seems like a Higher Power moment, a drop of the sergeant major's blood on a pin. He makes a crude mud statue and performs a ritual through which he hopes to give the sergeant major cancer. But then he has second thoughts, sees the bigger picture, deals with his resentments, and goes back on his pact. This script had much more interest: It was fresh and unique because it was drawn from my Memory Well, with some Imagination Well thrown in.

Even though it is a fantastic resource, the Memory Well also has its limitations. Few people are interested in our day-to-day life story, regardless of how interesting we think it is. Often when people in my workshops first learn about the power of memory writing, they start telling me, for example, about the time they went to an outdoor rave, took drugs, and had an amazing experience. Yes, that could be an interesting story, but the problem with focusing on our life stories alone is that if we indulge them and write only for ourselves, then we will lose focus and miss out on what writing is really about.

Writing films should be about reaching out and resonating. If we don't reach out, we can't connect with anyone. Accessing our memories to inspire us to write fresh and resonant stories is one thing, but narcissistically telling our—possibly boring—life story is another. Most of the moments in our lives are not cinematic and we should be careful of falling into the trap of self-indulgent writing from life.

Finally, it is important to remember that we don't have to draw our entire script from the Memory Well. We may be lucky enough to be employed to write, say, a superhero movie and have to invent a scene in a graveyard. Instead of letting our minds go to the External Sources or Imagination Wells, why not go to the Memory Well instead?

To write a fresh and authentic scene in a familiar genre such as a superhero movie, we can look back and use our past. I might recall my experience in the orange orchard. Can I have one of my superhero characters be buried back at the farm he grew up on? I could create a beautiful scene set in this cinematic and amazing location. It is still a superhero movie: it isn't my personal story. I am simply drawing on my memories to write a stronger and more meaningful scene. This way it becomes a scene unlike any other, because it contains the trace of one of my memories. It resonates.

THE GROUNDWATER

I hope that by doing the graveyard exercises you experienced the Three Wells distinctly. However, you may also feel that the wells are connected to one another. That is exactly where I want us to be. All the wells draw from the same groundwater. They trickle and seep into one another and they sometimes mix and swirl together within our writing.

We remember movies we have seen. Is that the Memory Well or the External Sources Well at work? When we recall a memory, we might recreate parts of it. Is that the Imagination Well or the Memory Well at work?

Even if we feel as if we are struck by a lightning bolt of an idea that comes out of nowhere, we may find that what we have imagined is linked to a life experience. Many years ago, an idea popped into my head for a children's story about a pink hippopotamus called Helga, which was subsequently published. It's a totally made-up story that takes place in an imagined world. The story came to me fully formed and in about ten minutes I had the bare bones structure and all the characters. It seemed to come purely from my Imagination Well. Years later I realized that it also tapped into my Memory Well, influenced by my own and others' experiences around addiction and body issues.

It seems that there is something at the heart of our imagination that comes only from our unique experiences. One of the myths about where stories come from is that a lightning bolt from above strikes us, perhaps even directly from Zeus. When lightning strikes it does indeed look as if it's coming from above. But the bright light we see is actually the energy pulsing back up to the sky. Objects on the ground are typically positively charged and when negative energy is released from the clouds it fans out in a series of very small, barely visible spurts. Only when the energy reaches an object on the ground and makes a connection is the strike sent heavenwards.

If we consider then the idea of Zeus striking from above, it is the exact opposite—the visibility of the strike originates from the receiver. The "strike from above" is personal. It's the positive charge within us that makes the strike visible. It may seem as if our imagined ideas come out of nowhere, but they come to us for a reason. As cognitive scientist Greg Nirshberg puts it: "Imagination is certainly a creative process, but it is only made possible by constructing an imaginative experience from stored fragments of memory that it can be built up from."

Research has shown that when men with amnesia were asked to imagine a scene, such as visiting a museum, and describe it with as much detail as possible, their imagined scenes were basic and primarily factual. But men without amnesia could imagine scenes much more vividly. So these tests affirm that our ability to recall memories is linked to our ability to imagine. The verdict is still out on this fascinating area of neuroscience, but for our purposes the link and the difference between the Memory and the Imagination wells is what is important.

The more we practice the techniques in this book, the more we will be able to recognize which well we are drawing from. We will start to notice the subtle differences between them and, at the same time, their even more subtle connections to each other.

WHICH WELL SHOULD I USE?

When writers start to consciously experience their wells, many become concerned about which one to draw their ideas from. Some writers are naturally connected to their memories. Some are very imaginative. Others are steeped in movie culture and find it easy to tap into their External Sources Well. As a result, people often ask me, "Which well is the best?"

The answer is that it depends on who you are and what you are writing. But I believe that for a story to really be emotionally fulfilling we must draw from all three.

Chances are that when we write, we are already drawing from our External Sources and Imagination Wells. But in order to become effective writers, we have to dig all three wells a little deeper. I challenge us to draw not only from one or two wells as we write, but to reach down and draw effectively from all three, particularly the often-ignored Memory Well.

If we know which well we are drawing from, we can consciously make sure we use all three. I have noted some of the limitations of the wells above. Now that you know them, you can look through your scripts to make sure that you aren't falling into any of the traps inherent in drawing from a single well.

For example, if I have written a great action thriller and know that I have drawn from the External Sources and Imagination wells, I might want to have another pass at the script while consciously drawing from my Memory Well. That way I can pepper the script with locations, emotions, and characters that are drawn from my unique life experience. We will learn how to do this in later chapters.

Or, if I have written a heartfelt drama based on an aspect of my life, I would have drawn from my Memory Well. I might have a look at the story again, looking for ways to insert some ideas from my Imagination or External Sources wells. I might want to change the story a bit and inflate a situation by using my Imagination Well. Or I might want to get ideas and inspiration from scenes or moments from movies I have watched. It also helps to consciously use the External Sources Well to make sure that we aren't unconsciously repeating ideas from other movies.

Ultimately, it is up to each individual writer to decide which well to use, and how often to use it. It will happen automatically. It is tempting to conjure up some matrix where I say that in order for a heist movie to be successful we need thirty percent External Sources Well, sixty percent Imagination Well and ten percent Memory Well. Or that for a coming-of-age TV drama series to work we need twenty percent External Sources Well, twenty percent Imagination Well, and sixty percent Memory Well. To some extent this kind of percentage is useful in that it illustrates how the wells can be integrated. However, I wouldn't dream about being so prescriptive around the writing process.

Drawing from the wells comes naturally to many writers. Regardless of your process, the following chapters will help you dig your wells deeper.

CHAPTER 2 EXERCISES

GRAVEYARD EXERCISE

1. Pretend that you have to write a funeral scene set in a graveyard.
2. Very quickly list some of the images that come into your head. Don't think too hard about it. Don't try to be original or imaginative. Just list images, ideas, or moments that instantly come into your head.

IMAGINED GRAVEYARD EXERCISE

1. Pretend you have to write a funeral scene set in a graveyard again. But this time, take a moment and access your imagination. Let your creative mind go wild and invent a graveyard scene.
2. List any new images, ideas, or scenarios that come to you.

GRAVEYARD FROM LIFE EXERCISE

1. Pretend you have to write a funeral scene set in a graveyard again. But this time take a moment and access your memories. Scan back through your life history. Think back to all the times when you may have been in graveyards. If you haven't been in one, you might think of one you have seen while driving past.
2. Make notes on the following. What did you see? Is there any particular graveyard experience that left a strong impression on you?
3. List some images, moments, or impressions that remain powerful in your mind.

CHAPTER THREE

DIGGING THE EXTERNAL
SOURCES WELL DEEPER

"I steal from every movie ever made."
— *Quentin Tarantino*

Knowing that we are drawing from the Three Wells when we create is a great start. If we can feel which well we are tapping into as we write, that's even better. But this is just the beginning. We should continue to improve and grow the further we progress on our writing journey. One part of this process is to dig our wells deeper to make sure they never run dry. Here's how.

Remember that the External Sources Well is more like a reservoir than a well. All movies, books, and any stories from the outside world are on tap, waiting for us to turn it on. We don't have to do much digging here. All we have to do is to watch more movies, read more books, and inhale more art and culture.

This does not mean simply watching our favorite TV series, although more power to us if filling our External Sources Well with new stories justifies binge viewing. Apparently Ingmar Bergman was "particularly fond of" watching Dallas in the evenings. If one of the most acclaimed art-house directors of all time filled his External Sources Well with mainstream TV, then there can be no harm in emulating him if we so desire. When we watch though, it can help to watch consciously knowing we are filling our External Sources Well for a specific reason.

WATCH BROADLY

Many writers who attend my workshops don't watch movies with enough variety. If our aim is to achieve authenticity and originality in our work, and if we draw from the same External Sources Well as other writers, we won't get there. So we shouldn't just watch the movies that the tabloids recommend or that have the flashiest previews. Hollywood is great at telling us which movies to see. Talk shows tell us that we must watch this or that. Billboards shout out films to passersby. Awards ceremonies tell us that this or that film is good and imply that we should watch them. Film is a consumer product and we are constantly told what to consume. Mostly we are told about typical mainstream films. Sure, we should watch those, but we need to broaden our range to succeed as writers.

That doesn't just mean we should only watch indie or foreign films from today. Many of my workshop participants haven't seen films that were made before the 1980s. For them, the '80s are light years away. We should watch older films, watch bad films, watch art films, watch experimental films, but most importantly, watch films that we aren't told to watch by the entertainment industry.

Turn to the end of this chapter and do the New Movie Exploration. This is one of the easiest explorations in this book. You will be asked to broaden your movie knowledge.

The famous magpie, Quentin Tarantino, constantly steals from other movies. You might have heard the story about how when he worked in a video store, he sat around watching obscure films. When he creates his films, he has a huge well to tap into and accesses water that seems fresh because it comes from obscure reservoirs. As far as I can tell, he doesn't forefront his Memory Well and we don't directly learn much about him from his films. Even so, some say he has created a new genre by simply mixing and matching from his External Sources Well. We will look in more detail at this collision of ideas in chapter 4, "Digging the Imagination Well Deeper." It doesn't take courage to tap into the External Sources Well, but it takes time and commitment to learn from movies that most other people haven't seen.

WATCH SPECIFICALLY

Just as it's important to watch broadly, it's also important to watch movies around the specific subject we are writing about. Another error many of my workshop participants make is that they become passionate about a specific story idea and dive into writing a script, and then, after months of work, they present it to the group. Someone inevitably points out that the story is just like some other film. The writer didn't research or watch any films around their story idea and ended up writing a film very similar to one that already exists.

To avoid this in your own writing, turn to the end of this chapter and do the Similar Movie Exploration exercise. This exercise only applies if you are currently working on a script or have a story idea you want to write. If you don't have one at this point, just keep reading. But my hope is that if you are reading this book, you do.

Sometimes when we write it feels as if we are tapping into the Imagination Well, unique ideas are flowing, and we are making everything up. It feels fantastic and original, but, in some cases, someone else has tapped a similar moment in their Imagination Well before and came up with something comparable to what we have. So, if we are writing a movie about football, we should make sure we fill our External Sources Well with as many sports movies or TV series as we can.

FROM STORY SLOTH TO STORY SLEUTH

As writers, we hardly ever have a day off. Just when I consciously decide to close my laptop and carve out some downtime on a Sunday morning, I open the newspaper and come across a story that speaks to me. Or I decide to mindlessly watch some YouTube clips and stumble across something stupid, but original, and I feel that there is a story there. It's just the way it works for me. We have to be open to stories around us that other people have collected already.

I like the idea of writers being story sleuths. We are like private investigators walking around with our magnifying glasses, looking for stories anywhere we can find them. Like detectives, some of us carry little notebooks around to take notes on story ideas rather than clues to a murder.

To explore this example and find your inner story sleuth, turn to the back of this chapter and do the Story Sleuth Exercise. This exercise is probably as old as writing courses themselves; in fact, you may have even done something like it before. The goal of the exercise is to remind you of the frequency with which we draw from the External Sources Well. Remember to be conscious of it.

If we are ever feeling stuck or uninspired, all we have to do is use exercises like this one to refill our External Sources Well. It can help us move from being uninspired story sloths to active story sleuths.

EXTERNAL SOURCES WELL AND RESONANCE

As I mentioned earlier, all the wells are connected. When we recall a film from our External Sources Well, we are also activating our memories. There were certain moments and images in the film that resonated with us. When we remember a story or article we read somewhere, we are drawing from the experience of reading the story and the emotion that came with it. It activated a neural pathway in our brain or spoke to our soul. Something about the film or the article stuck in our subjective memory.

It did this because of who we are, holding our entire accumulated unique life experiences. Other viewers or readers might not have noticed that moment in the film, or that story. But if it struck us, perhaps it will strike others if we reuse and reimagine it in our own scripts.

In this way, simply turning on the tap of the External Sources Well can help us achieve resonance because we remember specifically. The movies, scenes, and stories we recall say more about us as writers than they do about the movies themselves.

ADAPTATION

One of the most obvious ways to draw from our External Sources Well is by adapting a novel into a film script. There are a few fascinating aspects of this process that are worth looking at, particularly in relation to the Three Wells.

The first is that through the simple process of reading fiction to prepare to write the script, we activate both our External Sources and our Imagination Wells. When we read any book, fiction or nonfiction, the characters, events, and themes all enter our External Sources Well.

What's different about the process of reading as opposed to watching a film is that we have to activate our Imagination Well when we read. If a writer describes a room, they might choose to identify only a few objects. Our imagination fills in the rest of the picture. In a similar way, when depicting a character, a writer might only note a few facial features, stature, or an item of clothing. We as readers must flesh out the character in our minds. This is part of what makes reading so pleasurable. This is also one reason why people are often disappointed when they watch a movie based on a book they love. They have imagined the characters and locations in their own wells and when it doesn't match what is presented on screen, they are disappointed.

When adapting a novel it is critical to consciously know which well we are drawing from. If we want to stay close to the text, we are drawing from our External Sources Well. If we are happy to invent and embellish on the text, we will be drawing more from our Imagination Well.

For example, when we face the flashing cursor and get ready to write a character description, we can access our External Sources Well by looking through the book and directly copying the description. Or we can access our Imagination Well to expand on the description. It's important to feel when we are accessing our Imagination Well during this process so that we can remain true to the text if that is what we want to do.

To illustrate this in action, let's look at two very different adaptations. For the movie *No Country for Old Men* (2007), based on the Cormac McCarthy novel, Joel and Ethan Coen remained faithful to the text. In some ways, we could say that they relied heavily on their External Sources Well. Ethan Coen has said that while writing that film: "One of us types into the computer while the other holds the spine of the book open flat." The final film unfolds in a way that is, for the most part, incredibly close to the text of the novel.

In the film *Adaptation* (2002), Charlie Kaufman came upon on a very different approach when adapting Susan Orlean's *The Orchid Thief*. Kaufman is said to have had writer's block and eventually turned to his Imagination Well and created a fantastically imaginative and self-reflective story. The difference between the writing processes behind these two films illustrates, in a very simplistic way, the two wells in operation when it comes to adaptations.

We will look into how to access and develop our Imagination Well next. One of the easiest ways is to simply read more fiction. That way we can fill our External Sources Well and exercise our Imagination Well at the same time. What is interesting about the film *Adaptation* is that *The Orchid Thief* is a nonfiction book, so, in some ways, Kaufman was activating his Imagination Well by reading nonfiction, which will be one of the methods discussed in the next chapter.

CHAPTER 3 EXERCISES

NEW MOVIE EXPLORATION

1. Think back to a movie someone recently mentioned to you that you haven't seen yet, or a film you read about and want to see. Try to think of a film that is the type you wouldn't normally watch, something a little different from your normal cinema fair. Write down the film's title.
2. Brainstorm other films that you haven't seen and don't feel a massive urge to watch. This should be a film that you feel you really should watch but just haven't got around to yet. Write down the title.
3. Compile a list of at least ten feature films that you haven't watched and that are not typically the type of films you watch.
4. Watch some of these films. You don't have to finish this exploration right away, but make it your goal to finish the exercise within a few months. Start by watching one movie from your list this week.

SIMILAR MOVIE EXPLORATION

For this exercise, make sure you can get online to search the internet.

1. Choose a script or idea that you are working on. Do some googling around the subject of your script and see if you can identify other movies that address the same or similar subject. If your movie is about football, research other football movies. If your movie is a coming-of-age comedy set in

research other coming-of-age movies or simply
es set in suburbia.

a list of at least five movies that connect to your story
idea in some way.
3. Watch them. You don't have to watch these movies in
order to keep reading. Try and watch them over the next
few weeks.

STORY SLEUTH EXERCISE

For this exercise, make sure you have access to a newspaper
(online or printed).

1. Look through the newspaper and see if any article resonates
with you. Maybe it's a person profiled in an article. Maybe
it is a story about corruption, big business, or the environment that resonates with who you are now. Whatever it is, if
something moves you, make a note of it.
2. List a few characters, story ideas, or images that stuck with
you during your close exploration of the newspaper.
3. Keep this list for the Colliding Ideas Exercise at the end of
the next chapter.

CHAPTER FOUR

DIGGING THE IMAGINATION WELL DEEPER

"Imagination is like a muscle. I found out that the more I wrote, the bigger it got."
— *Philip José Farmer*

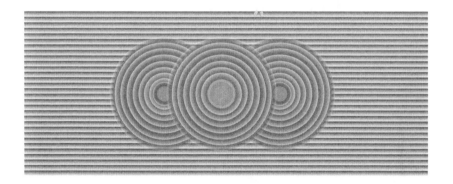

The Imagination Well is laid in fantastically porous soil. Once we access it, the ideas come shooting out like a geyser.

The challenge with this well is that often there is a hard stratum of rock that's been laid over the top of the soil. Simply stated, this rock is called "growing up." For many people, their imagination has slowly filtered away over years, and for some of us, our imagination was just kicked out of us. This chapter will introduce you to the Imagination Well, show you how it works, and help you dig it a little deeper. There are many paths through this hard layer of rock and it is up to you to discover which work best for you. Here are a few.

PLAY

My eight-year-old niece can keep herself busy for hours on end, inventing and creating whole worlds out of clothes pegs, pens, or whatever she has at hand. She needs little but her imagination to play.

Over the years, many books have been written to help us "free our inner child" and access our creativity. The most well known is Julia Cameron's *The Artist's Way*. My adult self riled against these books. I struggled for years with even the idea of being creative. It sounded so childlike and self-indulgent to me. Luckily, I got over that block because it is exactly this childlike energy that we tap into when we draw from our Imagination Wells. We all have the ability to play if we open ourselves up to it. Like reserved adults who have to join in a game with young kids, we may at first be reluctant, but soon we are imagining just as much as the children, connecting to their freedom of expression.

Some writers, especially those who are also actors, will get up from their laptops and fool around. They may perform scenes from their scripts. Some might recite lines while they sit. When I write, I mostly sit in silence or play music. However, if I am really stuck, I find that getting up and acting out the scenes helps ground me in my characters and the process often leads to new ideas popping up.

To experience the Imagination Well in action and to see how it is linked to physicality, go to the end of this chapter and complete the Object Experience.

How did the exercise feel? Were you able to get out of your head and just play?

This exercise forces us to spend time in our Imagination Well. Actors often use this exercise to develop their imaginations and there is no reason why we writers can't do the same. In fact, there are many acting tools we can employ in our creative process, some of which will be explored in chapter 8, "Acting for Writers."

Sometimes the easiest thing to do to access this well is to simply join kids in their games. If you have your own kids, nieces or nephews, or other children in your life, spend some time with them. Connect with them and their games. Let them lead and be guided by their imaginations. Experience the joy.

COLLIDING IDEAS

One of the simplest paths into the Imagination Well is through the External Sources Well and allowing the ideas, images, and characters there to stimulate our imagination. A way to do this is simply by combining ideas from the External Sources Well. Our minds often do this automatically and it's probably one of the most effortless forms of creativity.

Simply stated, colliding ideas is just a juxtaposition of two different things to create what feels like a new or imagined idea. When the two ideas collide, they can fuse or spark off new imagined ones.

To test this, turn to the back of this chapter and do the Colliding Ideas Exercise.

Did this exercise actively trigger your Imagination Well? Creative people collide ideas all the time. We create connections that other people don't see between images, characters, locations, scenes, and even genres.

An example of colliding genres would be the made-for-TV movie *Sharknado* (2013). The creators took the sharks from *Jaws* (1975) and tornados from natural disaster movies like *Twister* (1996) and mashed them together, even in the title, to create a story of sharks sucked up by a tornado and hurled at the innocent. A more classic example is *Alien* (1979), which was pitched as "*Jaws* in space." It's a combination of *Jaws* and space movies. Of course, it is also more than that because the filmmakers also drew from other parts of their Imagination Wells.

Simply colliding ideas can be a crude way of doing things and it might not result in the most original and fresh ideas. It depends on how deeply we have dug our External Sources Well and how we execute the integration of external sources and our imagination. If we have filled our External Sources Well by watching unique movies and make the ideas we have found there collide, we might come up with fantastically original ideas.

Remember that this technique should be used as a way of creating not only story genres, but also events, images, and characters. We will look at how to collide characters in chapter 7, "A Life of Characters."

INTELLECTUAL THOUGHT

In some ways this path into the Imagination Well is the polar opposite of play. Some writers access their Imagination Wells through intellectual thought. Filmmakers such as Stanley Kubrick and Werner Herzog seem to access their Imagination Wells in this way. We might even include others like the Wachowski siblings and some of Christopher Nolan's work in this group.

Their films are clearly imagined films that take place in worlds they, or their writers, make up. However, what separates these films from pure flights of fantasy is that they are centered on an intellectual premise. Movies like *The Matrix* (1999), *Inception* (2010), and *2001: A Space Odyssey* (1968) try to reach the cerebral in us. Their starting point, or the way I presume these filmmakers and writers accessed their Imagination Wells, was through intellectual thought.

Characters, situations, and scenes materialize as a result of thinking about life or science or politics or philosophy. The characters become representations of the theme. For example, in Werner Herzog's *Aguirre, the Wrath of God* (1972), each character represents an archetype around the theme of colonization. Herzog certainly knows how to tap into the other parts of his Imagination Well and his Memory Well, but he is also a cerebral filmmaker.

One of the most imaginative writers of all time was Lewis Carroll. He's the guy who wrote *Alice in Wonderland* and created exceptional nonsense verse. Most people have heard of him but not many know the deacon, logician and mathematician Charles Lutwidge Dodgson. Reverend Dodgson was a slightly tormented soul who was a practitioner of Victorian logic and reason. He suffered hours of melancholy, depression, and restless nights. Reverend Dodgson had extraordinary flights of fantasy and these materialized under the pen name . . . Lewis Carroll.

Often writers who have the most vivid imaginations are also very rational and logical people. It's as if they spend so much time thinking logically and rationally about the world that they build up steam like a pressure cooker. The Imagination Well is the pressure relief valve, which is why it can feel like a geyser of ideas escaping when we access it.

When I want to activate my Imagination Well, I dive into nonfiction books and films. If a particular subject interests me, I read about it and am open to the flights of fantasy that my mind goes on as a result of saturating it with facts and reason. I look for connections between ideas. I activate my "what if" imagination.

The "what if" principle is a simple method to get our imaginations going. All we have to do is think about one or more aspects of what we are reading. It could be a character or an event that we are reading about. Or it could be an intellectual idea that we want to explore. Then all we have to do is add "what if . . ." in our mind and see where our imagination takes us.

For example, at the moment I am reading a book entitled *We Are Anonymous* about the Anonymous computer hacking group. I might have a "what if" thought about hacking: "What if a hacker forces the president of a corporation to do . . . something." And there we have an idea from *Mr. Robot* (2015). Or if I'm reading about dream theory,

I might think: "What if I can enter someone's dreams?" And there we have the idea behind *Inception* (2010).

Turn to the back of the chapter and do the What If Exercise where you will be required to read some nonfiction and then activate your imagination around it.

Something to keep in mind when accessing the Imagination Well through intellectual thought and reason is that it can sometimes result in very cerebral films. We might end up with a film that operates purely on the intellectual level and it might not move people emotionally. Stanley Kubrick is one of my favorite directors and I love watching his films, but the experience is often a purely intellectual one. These films might operate on very visceral emotions, such as fright and disorientation in *The Shining* (1980) and humor in *Doctor Strangelove or: How I Learned to Stop Worrying and Love the Bomb* (1964), but overall the resonance of sharing from a lived life is missing for me. The same can be said of my experience of many of the other films mentioned above. Of course, the exception with Kubrick is that it seems his lived life was about structure and obsessive research. So we do learn about him through his films.

As mentioned in chapter 3, "Digging the External Sources Well Deeper," Charlie Kaufman's adaptation of *The Orchid Thief* into the fantastical *Adaptation* (2002) is another example of inspiring the Imagination Well through reading nonfiction.

If we do access our Imagination Well through intellectual thought only, our stories might benefit from drawing from our Memory Well and peppering our scripts with some moments drawn from life.

In this way we might achieve the personal resonance the audience is looking for.

SUFFERING, DEATH, AND THE DUENDE

Many theorists and artists have expressed a link between suffering and imagination. It is a complex notion that straddles both the Imagination and Memory wells. It's possible that we suppress our painful memories and then they "come out" in our imagination. Frederico García Lorca, the Spanish poet, speaks about the Duende in this respect. It is a particularly Spanish term and, as usual when writing about the source of creative ideas, it is a slippery concept. According to Lorca it can be understood as a "creature" that "targets beleaguered, tormented, suffering, struggling, or harassed artists, prompting them (in their desperate anguish and high anxiety) to heights of astonishing creative brilliance."

The Duende is also particularly Spanish because, says Lorca, "In every other country death is an ending. It appears and they close the curtains. Not in Spain. In Spain they open them. Tales of death and the silent contemplation of it are familiar to Spaniards."

It is understood as a vital impulse driving genuine and authentic creativity. And it resonates with the audience. It "comes from inside as a physical/emotional response to art. It is what gives you chills, makes you smile and cry as a bodily reaction to an artistic performance that is particularly expressive." The Duende is a "mystery, the roots that cling to the mire that we all know, that we all ignore, but from which comes the very substance of art."

It comes from experiencing suffering and death. These are hardships that we all have to endure in this life. They are a path into our Imagination Well.

A quick analysis of the origin of Lewis Carroll's nonsense poem *The Hunting of the Snark* illustrates this process. Some of Carroll's work has its origin not only in intellectual thought, but also in heartache and the Duende. On July 18, 1874, Margaret Wilkox sat up with Lewis Carroll's grandson, Charlie, until three in the morning when Carroll came to relieve her. He had called short a seaside holiday to help take care of Charlie, who had tuberculosis.

Carroll watched over his grandson until six in the morning, snatched a few hours sleep, and then went for a walk to clear his mind of the sick chamber. Carroll wrote that: "While I was walking on a hillside there suddenly came into my head one line of verse—one solitary line—'For the Snark was a Boojum, you see.' I knew not what it meant, then; I know not what it means now: but I wrote it down."

Within the next four days, in between intervals of nursing Charlie, Carroll worked on the final stanza of his poem. The final image of the poem was cathartic, conjured up in direct relation to his grandson's illness and impending death: "In the midst of the word he was trying to say/ In the midst of his laughter and glee/ He had softly and suddenly vanished away/ For the Snark *was* a Boojum, you see."

Carroll then created a whole world, characters, and journey to build up to this last stanza. In this way we can see a writer accessing the Imagination Well through heartache, death, and the Duende.

Just as the religious experience is a way of dealing with death and the randomness of life, so the imagination is a way in which we can cope with heartache. According to Lorca, if you are "seeking the Duende, there is neither map nor discipline." It is something we just experience.

David Lynch is a master of tapping this section of the Imagination Well. His first feature film, *Eraserhead* (1977), is a surreal story about a man whose girlfriend gives birth to a strange, bug-like creature. The film resonates with darkness and the Duende. Even though the story is drawn from the Imagination Well, it is interesting to note that Lynch possibly drew from the experience of his daughter being born with clubbed foot and having to undergo a series of corrective surgeries. The trauma Lynch probably experienced at this time seems to have worked its way into his story.

Now that we know of their creative power, we need to pay attention to moments of suffering or death in our lives, and notice how they can help us tap into our Imagination Wells.

THE ID

There is another fascinating connection between the Imagination Well and the Memory Well that is worth exploring. Some people are scared of what they will find when they let their imaginations run riot. They may worry about what it says about them, or their past, if they can create a terribly gory scene for a slasher film, for example. One theory of our imagination is that it's where our repressed id hides and so it makes sense that spending time there can be scary for some people.

According to Freudian theory, in broad strokes, our ego is held in check by our superego. That is the voice in our heads or society's rules that tells us that certain thoughts are bad and that certain experiences should be repressed. These "bad" thoughts and memories are then shoved into the id, which is like the basement of the self. It's where all our "bad" or "unsavory" ideas and drives are locked away.

One relatively easy way of accessing our Imagination Well is through wish-fulfillment fantasies. If we can't express our id in our daily life, we might end up writing about those repressed thoughts in our stories. Imagine if our boss fires us for no clear reason. We might want to respond and even punch them in the face. But we don't. Our superego tells us that society wouldn't like that so we repress the impulse and it is stored in our id.

Instead of acting out on that impulse, if we don't deal with the anger in some way, we might spend the next few days imagining how it could have played out differently. We could then write that into a scene where we end up blackmailing our boss and leaving with a year's pay, as expressed in similar scenes in *American Beauty* (1999) and *Fight Club* (1999).

If we are getting ready to go to a party, we might fantasize about what will happen there. We might picture having a really fun, wild time. Some of those thoughts might seem unsavory to our superego and they will remain unexpressed, and probably unful-filled, and then be locked in the id. We then might wish that things had played out differently. We might fantasize about a party going out of control, as expressed in almost any teen party movie or the whole of *Project X* (2012).

Most of the *Fast and The Furious* franchise comes right out of wish fulfillment. Very often movies about vengeance are also drawn from this well. Most of Tarantino's work, besides being mainly inspired by the External Sources Well, is about vengeance and is this kind of wish-fulfillment fantasy.

Countless movies have been made drawing from this section of the Imagination Well. Very often these movies are either violent or overtly sexual in nature. The viewer gets a kick out of watching them, and the writer probably gets a kick out of writing them. The audience may enjoy seeing someone on screen behaving in a way they wish they could. Perhaps it is a moment in the film when a worker beats his boss into a pulp or a spouse has an affair with a hot lover. In that moment, anyone in the audience who has had those fantasies will likely be enjoying the film as they watch them play out on the screen.

It can be enjoyable and almost cathartic for the viewer. This specific experience, though, is not the resonance I mentioned earlier, at least not in the way I am referring to it. The fantasy on screen echoes just what it is: a fantasy. Enjoyable, but what does it really tell us about living and feeling in the real world?

The problem with writing an entire film using wish-fulfillment fantasy is that if we as writers haven't actively looked into our own lives and faced our shadows, we might end up writing something that we didn't intend to. The movies might be fun. They may be harmless, but they can also lead us, and our audience, astray.

Here is a concrete example. A few years ago I wrote a slasher horror film. It is about a group of students on their way to an outdoor rave in the desert who take a wrong turn, break down, and then slowly but surely get hacked to death by a pickaxe-wielding scientific experiment gone wrong and fed to his two genetically modified dogs. I was drawing from the Three Wells. Firstly, I would say it was about thirty percent drawn from the External Sources Well, inspired by *The Hills Have Eyes* (1977) and other slasher movies. I drew about sixty percent from the Imagination Well. And I would say there was probably only about ten percent from the Memory Well. The script got development funding and was sold to a production company. All seemed well. When looking at the process from a distance, however, I learnt an interesting lesson.

I had adhered to the genre conventions and so ended up writing a film full of violence, sex, and titillation. The message of the film ended up being: "Don't go into the wilderness or you will get killed and eaten!" I love the wilderness, and this is the furthest from what I want to say as a writer. So where did this story come from? Just before I wrote the script I was teaching at a film school. I was overworked as I was lecturing cinematography, editing, and sound design and was also running the post-production studio and the gear house. I had stretched myself too far. As a result I had a lot of misdirected resentment toward the film school that I hadn't worked out of my system. My repressed anger came out in the script. It was, after all, about a bunch of students being hacked to death!

Now, there is nothing inherently wrong with writing a slasher if that's what we are into, but, for me, I didn't want to send that message. I had let my wish-fulfillment fantasy run away with me. I have discovered that the more I find out about myself as a person and a writer, the easier it becomes to recognize when fantasy and imagination are steering me away from what I really want to say.

I'm saying two seemingly contradictory things here. The first is that we shouldn't judge ourselves when we use our id to access our Imagination Well. We shouldn't be afraid of what we will find there. We should boldly go and explore our Imagination Well in our vomit drafts without any moral judgment.

The second is that if we want to be clear about what we want to say with our films, we can edit our thoughts, or the whole story, in the rewrite. If we discover that what we have written doesn't add to the world in the way that we expected, we can change the story.

Also, the more we get to know ourselves, through accessing and dealing with repressed thoughts and memories, the clearer our writing will become. The repressed id is like a stagnant pool: The more we can clearly access our memories, the more we can filter it, and the easier it is to draw from.

Finally, having said all of that, it's just writing. It has been said that, "screenwriting isn't rocket science, it's harder." There's probably some truth to that. But screenwriting also isn't brain surgery. No one's life is at stake if we write a violent scene or if we develop a script that doesn't work. Even if our whole script is a flight of fantasy, so what? Often our creativity is stifled because we feel that we have to write a politically correct script. We should drop that attitude. Have fun with it. Enjoy the process and the ideas will flow easier.

EXTERNAL SOURCES TAINTING THE IMAGINATION WELL

Earlier I mentioned my niece. When I watch her play I see how her External Sources Well sneaks into her Imagination Well. She loves YouTube and at the moment she is obsessively watching a particular animated series. The characters and scenes slowly slip into her games. Now when she plays she uses characters, dialogue, and situations like the ones she's seen in that series. Phrases, words, and scenarios from the series work their way into her imagined world. I'm sure we've all seen this happen with kids and it can be a wonderful thing. But as creators, we need to be hyperaware of when this happens to us.

It happened to me in a way that seems so unlikely that I want to share it here. I was directing a film in which there was a scene set in the back room of a gun store. The character sits aligning the sights of a rifle. When we were location scouting I noticed that just behind the gun racks there was a toaster. It was such an unlikely kitchen implement in this rather dark and cluttered workspace. I imagined a scene where the character is carefully adjusting the sights and then just before we cut away from the scene there is a loud popping sound as some toast, which had been toasting all the while, pops up. It was an unexpected and funny moment that broke the tension of the scene.

Some time after shooting it I was re-watching *The Graduate* (1967) and there is a similar beat in that film. Benjamin tells his parents that he's going to marry Elaine and they are ecstatic at first, but gradually realize that he hasn't asked her yet. Their bubble bursts and, as Ben exits, a toaster pops up in the foreground, breaking the tension. I had seen the film once or twice many years before and clearly the moment stayed in my External Sources Well. When I thought I was drawing only from my Memory Well of experience (the location scout) and my Imagination Well (making up the moment in the film), I was also drawing from my External Sources Well.

This is not the end of the world. There is a lot to be said for referencing other films but it should, ideally, be done knowingly, or else we might find ourselves simply copying without knowing it. If we are on a quest for authentic and original stories, we need to be hyperaware of when our Imagination Well is being tainted by our External Sources Well.

CHAPTER 4 EXERCISES

OBJECT EXPERIENCE

As with most of the experiences in this book, there is no right or wrong here. There is just the experience.

1. Look around and pick up any object. Make sure that it isn't too delicate. It could be a plastic water bottle, a piece of wood, or a teacup. Anything. Don't think about it—just pick something up. Anything except your cell phone that is!
2. Stand up and hold the object in your hand.
3. Using your whole body, act using the object. If, for example, it is a water bottle, indicate drinking out of it.
4. Now access your Imagination Well and pretend the object is something else. Act using the "new" object. For example, a water bottle might be a telescope. Indicate looking through it as if it was a telescope. Importantly, the object can become anything at all. A water bottle could be a baby, a baseball bat, a TV remote, or even a ticking bomb. Whatever you choose, make sure that you use your whole body when you act. Try to imagine five different things that the object in your hand could be. If you like, you can use your voice to make sound effects or invent dialogue. Have fun!
5. Take this a step further and shorten the duration between your new objects. Don't allow your object to remain one thing for more than five seconds; move your imagination on quickly to turn the object into something else. When you feel that you have run out of ideas of what the object could be, push it further.

COLLIDING IDEAS EXERCISE

1. Get the list you made after doing the Story Sleuth Exercise at the end of chapter 3.
2. Randomly select two of these ideas, images, events, or characters and make them collide. For example, if you have found a story about political corruption, combine it with anything at all, maybe even a photo of a cute puppy.
3. Activate your Imagination Well. Can you find a connection between the two ideas? Is there a story there?
4. Repeat steps 2 and 3 using different ideas, images, or objects on your list.

WHAT IF EXERCISE

1. Find some nonfiction to read. It could be a newspaper, but ideally it is longer than a newspaper article. A featured article in a magazine would be good or even a nonfiction book.
2. Read the piece of nonfiction for a while. Even if it takes you an hour, that is fine. While you are reading, though, I want you to consciously feel your Imagination Well being stimulated.
3. Once you have finished reading, use the "what if..." principle (discussed in this chapter's section titled Intellectual Thought).
4. Write down any ideas for characters, images, or plots that might have come to you.

CHAPTER FIVE

DIGGING THE MEMORY WELL DEEPER

"Write what should not be forgotten."
Isabel Allende

The Memory Well is dug into hard, unyielding desert rock. Memory writing can be one of the most difficult things to do. But we will see, like a spring in the desert, it's the sweetest, freshest, and most satisfying water we can find. Digging deeper into this often ignored well is important. If you can learn to access this well, to go deeper, and to use this to shape your writing, my work is done.

Just like with the Imagination Well, there are a few books that can help us access our memories to make our writing better, like *Story Line* by Jen Grisanti. I am surprised that there aren't more books on this topic. In workshops, as soon as we begin tapping this well, participants start engaging in a different way. It is a very powerful moment for all of them. Tears flow. Laughter fills the air. The room becomes a place of true creativity and healing.

It's also a fragile space.

Before you begin these exercises, make sure that you have support. A loved one to call. Someone to speak to. These exercises are powerful and potentially transformative, so don't take them lightly. If workshop facilitators plan to use this book, they should make sure that they create a safe space for their participants.

This well contains all the emotions of our past experiences—turmoil, death, pain, and truth, as well as humor, joy, and love. To dig this well deeper, we need to protect ourselves, make sure that we wear some kind of emotional safety gear, and yet try to remain open at the same time.

MEMORY AND THE SENSES

Before we start these exercises, an important word about memory and the five senses.

When we recall our memories, I want us to truly place ourselves in that exact moment in space and time. To do this, I suggest that we use our five senses. What did the place look like where the memory occurred? What did it smell like? Are there any tastes associated with the memory? What were we touching at the time? What were the sounds that we heard?

When it comes to recalling memories, sound and taste are particularly evocative. We respond emotionally to music or voice. Either can activate our memories. Smell is intensely powerful because it is the one sense that bypasses the thalamus, which is the area in the brain that is like a filter between our sensory organs and our cortex where we process impulses. When we sleep, the thalamus "switches off," which is why when we are in deep sleep soft sounds or a light touch won't wake us up. Smelling salts are used to wake up people who are passed out because of this. Smell is one of the primary ways to access repressed memories and emotions.

Film is an aural as well as visual medium. One of the easiest and most immediate ways to create emotional resonance for the audience is through sound. This is because humans respond emotionally to sounds long before we respond to images.

By week twenty-four of a pregnancy, a fetus can turn its head in response to sounds. So we spend the last three months in the womb floating in a sea of sound. Arguably, we hear the rhythm of stories and dialogue while we are still in the womb. Once we are born we can see about one-hundred-and-eighty degrees in front of our face, but the world of sound constantly surrounds us. We can close our eyes, but it is more difficult to close our ears. We might hear a sound first and then identify it. We hear a thump in the night and then whip around to identify the source of the sound with our eyes.

What is important here is that people have an emotional response to sound and then an intellectual response based on what they see. We might be fearful if we hear a crash in the dead of night when we are alone in an empty house. We might feel joy if the sound is a child laughing. This is a powerful tool for filmmakers. Sound designers and editors know this and use it all the time. Screenwriters should do the same.

It's okay if we can't access all our senses when we recall a memory. The point here is that our memories will be active and alive for us when we use our senses to recall them. They should be vibrant. If we can access that vibrancy and transform it into a scene or a moment in a film, then we can inject the vitality of that memory directly into our scripts and make them come alive.

THE FIRST MEMORY

I would like us to recall our earliest memory. You may ask why I want to go back to such an early memory. One of the reasons is that our early life experiences inform so much of our writing. As Willa Cather puts it, "Most of the basic material a writer works with is acquired before the age of fifteen."

With this particular exercise, some people can't figure out if what they recall is an actual memory or something that someone else told them about that became their memory. For example, I have a "memory" that I am not too sure about. I have watched a grainy home movie of myself as a baby. I was in a cot. Hanging above me was a mobile made of strange, blue plastic birds. In a flash, I had a "memory" of seeing those birds from my own baby point of view. I recalled reaching out and trying to touch them, but never being able to. I even recalled the taste of the metal springs attached to the birds. Now, I don't know if that memory was real or if I imagined it after watching the home movie, but the point is that, either way, it's a fresh idea for a scene or a prop.

Don't worry too much about where the memory comes from right now. Remember that all the wells mix together. With all these memory exercises we just need to be sure that we tap into something that feels authentic to us.

So what is your first memory? Turn to the end of this chapter and do the First Memory Exercise.

My earliest memory that I am sure of is of crawling on the floor of our kitchen and seeing a colorful caterpillar. It was one of those hairy caterpillars. I reached out to touch it. I grabbed it and my little hand was covered in itchy spikes. I cried.

That's about all I can remember, but the moment is crystal clear in my mind. I can still see the worm crawling up from the linoleum floor and onto the brown wooden back door, which had scratches on it from the dog wanting to go outside. I can feel my childlike curiosity and the spikes against my hand. This is not an earth-shattering memory, but it could be a beautiful moment in a film.

Now go back to your own first memory. Is it something you have seen in a movie before? That's unlikely. After all, it's your memory. Even if other people have had similar memories and experiences, and even if they have been represented on the screen, the point is that this one is yours alone. It might be a traumatic memory. It might be a funny one. It might be completely random, but if you can really place yourself in that time and space and activate your senses, you will probably find that you could create a scene, or a moment in a scene, that is truly one of a kind.

This is how drawing from the Memory Well works. And this is only the beginning.

FOUR MEMORIES

If you did the First Memory Exercise, you are starting to dig a deeper hole for your Memory Well. Your first memory is the first chink in the rock. Can you feel how you had to access a totally different part of your brain here than when accessing the External Sources and Imagination wells? Can you see that it was a challenge to truly recall your memory, but, once you had it, you could prob-ably bring the memory to life in a really singular way?

It takes time and practice to successfully draw from the fresh waters found at the bottom of this well.

But it's worth it.

So let's keep going.

You may want to take a break between these exercises. Get up and prepare yourself a hot or cold drink. Go for a walk. Take some time to reflect. It might prime you for the next exercise.

Movies take us on a roller-coaster ride of ups, downs, highs, lows, climaxes, and endings. When we recall a movie, we see it in moments. Looking back through our own lives is a bit like remem-bering a movie. We won't be able to recall each and every moment, but we will be able to remember events that left an imprint on us. When we look back, we will be able to skip to certain moments, like when we skip through a movie. We create new memories every day and our brains can't possibly store each and every one, so we forget some; we bundle others together. Memory is slippery.

To navigate our way into our memories I have identified specific memory moments that I would like us to skip to. We are going to look at our saddest memory, our angriest memory, our happiest memory, and a memory from today.

SADDEST MEMORY

One of my saddest memories is from when my father passed away. It is a complex memory because he was fighting a long battle with cancer and so there was even some relief in the moment. Expressing the complexity of human emotions is what makes films ring true. Being able to express those layered feelings on film is real gold.

Now it's time to be brave. For some people in my workshops this is a very challenging memory to write about. After the first memory, we're jumping into the deep end, but there is method to this. If we want to write deeply, and we want to go on this journey, then this is like crossing the threshold. We've got to do it and go for it one-hundred percent or not do it at all.

Can you recall your saddest memory, or at least a very sad moment? Do the Saddest Memory Exercise at the end of this chapter.

After doing the exercise, have a look at the memory experience you have described. Is it something that you have seen in a movie before?

As mentioned earlier, in my memory of my father's death, there is a feeling of sadness, but also cathartic release. I was driving alone in my car to his house after I had heard that he had just passed away. He lived in a small coastal suburb, accessible via a short mountain pass. It is a main thoroughfare so there were quite a few cars, but the road travels through a nature reserve, so to the left and right of me was wilderness. I looked into the rear-view mirror and two cars back I noticed my brother's car. He was also on his way.

As we were driving, I saw a black dog on the side of the road, trotting around, looking about frantically, clearly lost. I pulled over, as did my brother. He got out of his car and the dog ran toward him and he tried to catch it, but it slipped past him. Cars zoomed by. I also got out of my car. We were silent, but we both knew that we wanted to see if we could find its tag or help rescue the dog. It ran toward me and I crouched down. I tried to call it but it totally ignored me: it just kept trotting past and headed up the road. "No tag," I shouted to my brother. He shrugged. What could we do? Even if we caught the dog we wouldn't know whom it belonged to. We would have to take it to a shelter, and we had to get back to the house to be with our mother. So we got back into our cars and drove on. It seemed like the dog knew where it was going anyway.

So there we have it. A scene. A moment. A sad moment, but also a moment that is poetic and already full of symbolism.

I might have been able to make up a scene like that, but it's unlikely. If I were writing about two brothers on their way to their dead father, I don't think a scene like that would come to me from my External Sources or Imagination wells. But, by accessing the Memory Well, I could now harness some of the feelings, images, and events from that time and rework them into a touching scene in a film.

Look back at your own sad memory that you have identified. How would you write the emotion of that moment into a scene? Is there an image or sound that you can use? Did you stare at the branch of a tree blowing in the wind? Was it raining? Did you hear a tin roof popping in the hot sun? Were there any real and authentic moments you can reuse in your work?

Take a short break before doing the next exercise.

ANGRIEST MEMORY

It's time for one more challenging exercise before we put some balm on the wound with a happiest memory exercise.

Anger, I find, is a simple emotion and one that clearly punctu- ates one's life. Many of my workshop participants find it easy to remember moments when they've been angry, even if they didn't express it at the time. When I did this exercise, I literally skipped through my life, noticing little peaks of anger here and there.

While anger seems like a simple emotion, as writers we have to think carefully about how we use it in our stories. To up the stakes of a boring scene, writers in my workshops often just make their characters cross with one another and, before you know it, they're having a screaming match. I think it's as a result of misun- derstanding the common piece of writing advice that "all drama is conflict."

To create conflict, some writers make their characters angry and create a husband and wife screaming in the kitchen scene. Or a teenage girl and mother screaming in her bedroom scene. Or busi- ness partners arguing in the boardroom scene. These scenes are found in many films. When done well, they engage us and hold our attention, possibly because we want to be able to express our anger like that in the real world.

When done badly, they are unconvincing and lack the subtleties of real-life conflict, which is often not as direct and on the nose. So even though it can be cathartic for some audience members to live through the anger expressed in movies, we may want to be cautious about expressing anger too quickly or too blatantly in our films. It might not ring true to life.

There are three main reasons for using our angriest moments. First, it can be relatively easy to remember when we were angry. Second, I want us to see how, in life, many of us express anger very differently than the clichéd ways portrayed in some movies. And the third reason is that if we can get in touch with what makes us angry, we might be a step closer to getting in touch with the themes and issues we want to write about. This way we can transform our anger through our writing. We will come back to this later in chapter 6, "Finding Your Theme."

At this point, turn to the end of this chapter and do the Angriest Memory Exercise.

Once you have done the exercise, check yourself. How are you feeling? Are you resonating with your anger? Do you feel any regret that you didn't express yourself more in that moment? At this stage in my workshops, a lot of unexpressed anger pops up in the room. We must be sure to draw a line between this exercise and our daily lives. We could meditate, pray, walk, or do whatever it is that helps us stay balanced. I want us to use the past in our work in the present, but I don't want the memories that we are accessing now to negatively affect our everyday lives.

I have experienced many angry moments and in almost all of them I didn't express my anger. So I am choosing to share a memory when I did express my anger. One of the things that really gets my goat is littering. There is something so selfish about people thoughtlessly chucking trash into the world that it drives me mad. When I was younger, I lived near a wetland. It was relatively untouched by development. There was a river that flowed into a small lagoon. It felt like a sanctuary, filled with birds like pelicans, flamingos, and even the occasional fish eagle. But inevitably, the developers came. Over time, the area became the fastest-growing suburb in the Southern Hemisphere.

As a kid, I used to take walks into the wetland alone. One quiet Sunday, as I was out walking, I turned a corner and saw that a whole swath of wetland had been flattened to make way for housing. Waterbirds were hopping about on the ground, chirping while looking for their nests, which had been destroyed. There was no one around as I crept further into what was still left of the wetland. In a small clearing next to the river a large billboard had been dumped in the water. It was an advertisement for the new development. I was so enraged that I grabbed the nearest log and started bashing the sign. Water splashed around me with each blow, but I blindly kept thrashing away until the sign was in pieces. At one point I heard a noise, turned around, and locked eyes with two fishermen innocently walking past. I don't know how much they saw, but they backed away without a word from what I presume was a red-faced, crazy-looking, half-drenched, feral child.

It's a tragic scene but also funny because of the witnesses to the rage, the two fishermen. I like this memory and it is something I could use in my writing. I haven't seen it in a film before.

Reflect on your angriest memory. Have you seen a moment like that in a film? If so, how is yours different? I bet that if you focus on the differences, you'll find a fresh and amazing moment that you can use.

Remember that it's not the exact memory I want us to write about in our scripts necessarily. It's the actions, sounds, scenes, and characters that make up those moments that are charged with an energy, which is potent when we remove it from our memories and plug it into our scripts.

HAPPIEST MEMORY

A movie is essentially a series of moments, some high and some low, in an order that is pleasing to an audience. To get our audience to feel the low points of our films, we also need to take them up to the high points.

The New Zealand film *Once Were Warriors* (1994) is a bleak but ultimately inspiring tale about domestic abuse set in a Maori community. It is written with such clarity and authority that it is unsurprising that the original book, written by Alan Duff, is informed by Duff's troubled childhood and is drawn directly from his Memory Well. Even though a lot of the film focuses on traumatic memories, there are also moments of lightness. These balance out the film and make the family dynamic at the center of the story seem authentic.

One such moment is when the family is about to set out on a road trip to visit the son, who is at a home for troubled boys. The abusive alcoholic father says, "Visits don't start till after lunch, we might as well take a drive, hey kids." The other siblings cheer and they drive away in their hired car, moving away from the urban sprawl and into the picturesque countryside. A track plays on the radio. The whole family breaks out into song, led by the father. The family is all smiles. The sun is shining. The grass is green. Life, for now, is good.

Even though the moment could play as forced, it resonates with authenticity. It's not an unrealistic or extreme high. The family hasn't won the lottery. It's a small, closely observed moment. It helps that the song playing on the radio is "What's the Time Mr. Wolf," which resonates with the theme of the film. The father is the wolf: an unpredictable alcoholic who at any point can turn domestic bliss into violent dinnertime.

This is a low-scale happiest moment compared to other films where the high points are almost impossibly high, such as surfing on the roof of a car, getting your own TV show, or winning millions. We, the audience, live vicariously through cinematic moments like these. But they are often overly dramatic, almost unbelievable high points. The happiest moment of an average life is probably not as cinematic as most filmmakers would want to depict in their films.

In life, many of us don't have a high like serving an ace to win Wimbledon or catching a long pass in the final seconds of the last quarter to help our team win the Super Bowl. However, the happiest moment in an average life is as important as these momentous highs for the person living that life. Even if it's a tiny moment, it's ours, it's real, and the emotions can be worked into any similar moment in a script. This will be discussed further in chapter 8, "Acting for Writers," under the heading Substitution.

Interestingly enough, many people attending my workshops have difficulty accessing their happiest memory. That doesn't surprise me. It seems easy for us to focus on the sad or angry moments of our lives. They feel heavier and seem to leave more of an imprint. Many of us are blessed to live mostly happy lives. Identifying one moment of pure happiness can be difficult. It's why making gratitude lists is such a powerful thing. It reminds us of all the joys in our daily lives that we often take for granted.

Turn to the end of this chapter and do the Happiest Memory Exercise.

One of my happiest memories is a simple one. I was in my mid-twenties and was sailing in a dinghy on a dam while a close friend skippered. There were no other sailboats about. The wind was just perfect and we were flying across the water. I was out on trapeze. I held the sail rope in my teeth as I pulled it in and I remember how it tasted of water. It was a sunny day and warm water was spraying everywhere.

At the one end of the dam there were these old rotting trees that jutted out of the water. Years ago, when the dam was filled, the trees were mostly covered by the water. Only a few large black trunks and branches stuck out of the water and scraped the sky. My friend steered us toward a small gap between two of the trees. The sailboat barely fitted between them. In that moment I felt exhilarated, happy, and free. I am sure that I shouted with joy.

There are other moments I can think of and that particular moment is perhaps more a moment of exhilaration than a conventional happy one, but as we are seeing, emotions are not as fixed as that. That's what makes them interesting. "Happy" can have several meanings and look several different ways. The sailboat moment is not over-the-top happy, but it's not something I have seen in a movie, and it would make a fresh and interesting scene. Have a look at your happiest memory. If you were to write it as a scene, do you think that your happiness would resonate with the audience watching the film?

At this point I want to go back to Van Gogh and my experience in the museum. The painting *Wheatfield with Crows* resonated with me at the time because it is a dark painting. It is commonly known as the last one Van Gogh painted before he shot himself. It is linked to the notion of the Duende mentioned in chapter 4, "Digging the Imagination Well Deeper."

My other memory of the art works in that museum was that his sunflower paintings were literally oozing yellow joy and happiness into the room. I'm sure that Van Gogh loved sunflowers. The joy and happiness he felt when painting them spills out into the gallery and one can see people basking in Van Gogh's radiant happiness. The resonance is clear. He found a way of communicating his happy feeling across decades.

Check yourself. How do you feel right now after recalling your happiest moment? Does the room feel lighter? Does your heart resonate with the memory when you recall it? Do you think you could communicate that emotion in a script?

MEMORY FROM TODAY

One of the remarkable things about the Memory Well is that it's inexhaustible. Once we break through the rock strata above this well and start to recall our memories, we find that we are experiencing unique moments and creating new memories all the time. As we go through our day, things happen that, if we are open to them, are often surprisingly interesting and exceptional.

To illustrate this point I want us to recall a moment today that was out of the ordinary or stood out in some way.

Chances are that if we are living the average life of a writer, we haven't consciously experienced any significantly memorable events today. Perhaps you chose to take this book with you on your solo ascent of Everest. If so, then something memorable probably happened. Or maybe you woke up, stayed in bed, reached over and started reading this book. If you have lived just another day in your life without any high or low moments, then you will have to comb carefully through your day to do this exercise.

It's a common expression that life passes us by. We passively let it pass. We go through our daily routine. Our minds gloss over the ups and downs of the day. If we look closely and zoom into the tiny moments, though, we will notice subtle ups and downs.

This exercise is a small one, but it's a very important one. We most likely won't find an earth-shattering moment in this exercise, but the goal is to practice. We can learn to explore our own lives with the precision of a scientist looking through a microscope. It's not easy and it may take some time, but let's look at a moment from today.

Do the Memory from Today exercise at the end of this chapter. Try to recall a small but out-of-the-ordinary moment that you experienced today.

I woke up this morning and it was a chilly 37 degrees Fahrenheit outside. There was a large amount of condensation on the windows. So that the house doesn't get too damp, I have taken to mopping down the glass windows in our entrance hallway with a towel first thing every morning. I stand there in my white dressing gown, my breath pluming from my mouth and run a towel up and down these full-length glass windows. The towel gets colder and wetter in my hands the more I wipe. I hear early morning birds call from vivid green trees. The windows are so high that I have to squat down and then jump up to reach the top. From the outside it must look like I'm doing some bizarre early morning exercise.

That moment is random in my life. But, again, it isn't something that I have seen in a movie. It reminds me of the scene in *Fargo* (1996) where Jerry is scraping ice off his windshield and then, because he's under pressure, explodes in an impotent fit of rage and then just goes back to the task of scraping off the ice. I suspect that this scene was inspired by real life. Depending on how I choose to write my memory it could be funny, tragic, or simply the routine motions of a morning, but it will certainly be fresh and unique.

Look back at the moment you came up with. Even if it seemed totally bland, if you really put yourself in the moment and extract the specific emotions around it, I am certain that you will have a scene that hasn't been depicted in a film.

Remember that our quest here is for specific resonance. We are looking for scenes, moments, or emotions from our lives that are unique and will resonate with an audience.

These moments are passing us by all the time. In order to dig our Memory Well deeper, our job, from now on, is to notice them.

THE SUBTLETY OF EMOTIONS

For the purposes of getting us to easily access our Memory Wells, I've chosen emotional states that are fairly simple to understand and identify. Sadness, Anger, and Happiness are very common and all relatively simple on the surface.

Some other emotions worth exploring are:
Joy
Fear
Regret

Pleasure
Heartbreak
Shame
Desire

It is worth repeating that the emotions we experience in life are not one-dimensional and fixed. Truthfully, if we look closely, they can't be reduced to one word. We could write a film that maintains a simple understanding of emotions. For example, we could have a film peppered with simple characters that experience pure happiness or pure sadness. But using only these one-dimensional expressions of emotions will result in a one-dimensional story.

What are more interesting are those moments where seemingly contradictory emotions bleed into one another. Like the moment of sadness and relief I felt at my father's passing. Or a moment when desire and shame meet. Or when fear and joy coexist.

The animated film *Inside Out* (2015) illustrates this simply but effectively. Each emotion that the character experiences is represented as a ball of a single color and is categorized separately in her memory. As she grows up she learns that the emotions are not that simple and they merge to become multi-colored balls.

Spend some time identifying moments in your own life when you felt a mixture of emotions. What were they? Accessing those moments, and effectively communicating them on screen, is what will make our films resonate with the complex truth of life. The result will be a window into the way we experience the world.

Van Gogh knew this instinctively. His sunflowers, so filled with joy and happiness, are very sad at the same time.

OBSERVE LIFE

Another way of digging the Memory Well deeper is to watch the world around us and to live in the moment. This is very Zen and, for many people, it is the point of life. To be present and live in the moment is a challenge that people spend a lifetime trying to achieve. We need to be present in the world in order to dig our Memory Well deeper.

Some writers I know are so sensitive to the world that they go to the other extreme and isolate themselves in their writing rooms. We need to be careful of closing ourselves off from the moments that happen around us every day. We shouldn't let script-worthy events and characters slip past us.

In his seminal work on acting, *An Actor Prepares*, Konstantin Stanislavski describes such a moment from his own life, which is worth quoting in full:

"Let me tell you about an old woman I once saw [activating the Memory Well in the present] trundling a baby carriage along a boulevard. In it was a cage with a canary. Probably the woman had placed all her bundles in the carriage to get them home more easily. But I wanted to see things in a different light [activating the Imagination Well], so I decided that the poor old woman had lost all her children and grandchildren and the only living creature left in her life was this canary. So she was taking him out on a ride on the boulevard, just as she had done, not long before, her grandson, now lost. All this is more interesting and suited to the theater than actual truth. Why should I not tuck that impression into the store-house of my memory? I am not a census taker, who is responsible for collecting exact facts. I am an artist who must have material that will stir my emotions."

Stanislavski was open to life. He was constantly observing the world around him, tucking the "impression(s) into the storehouse of (his) memory." He was always on the lookout for characters and moments that he could draw from, actively engaging with life, as a director, actor, or writer should.

In this example, Stanislavski makes the important distinction between factual memory and emotional memory. For him, it is more important to learn emotional truths from one's engagement with the world. The old woman he was watching probably didn't lose her whole family, but Stanislavski uses the memory to spark off an emotion, which stirs him, and, if retold or performed, should resonate with others.

Being open to the world in this way goes against how many of us have learnt to live. We are so busy getting through our days that we don't stop and look around us. We stare at our smartphones and read our iPads on the bus rather than looking into people's eyes and nodding hello. It's easier just to put our heads down and charge through life. Often we become more and more closed off from the world. Life can be hard. We build walls to protect ourselves.

What I'm asking us to do is to look up and fully experience and observe the world around us.

According to the book *Daily Rituals* by Mason Currey, Charles Dickens found time to write in a very healthy manner. He would write in absolute quiet from 9 a.m. to 2 p.m. Then he would walk around London from 2 p.m. to 5 p.m. In the evening, he would spend time with family, have dinner, and sleep. Those three hours walking the streets of London were vital to his work and it's clear he was filling his Memory Well with fantastic characters and events that he saw. We too could start to dig our Memory Wells deeper by filling them with people, places, and things we experience.

Enriching the Memory Well in this way goes far beyond the art of writing, and ultimately becomes the art of living.

PRIMARY RESEARCH AND THE MEMORY WELL

There are two kinds of research: primary research and secondary research. Secondary research is based on information gathered by others. We experienced this kind of research during the Story Sleuth exercise when we read the newspaper. In chapter 4, "Digging the Imagination Well Deeper," we saw how we can access parts of our imagination through reading nonfiction or watching documentaries made by others. This is all secondary research.

Primary research is new research. It could be interviews we have personally conducted or photographs we have taken. It is preferable to secondary research because it is new and personal. If we do primary research for our stories by physically going to the place our film is set, or actively engaging with the kinds of people we are writing about, we begin to directly experience the world of our stories. We create memories around that real space. We fill our Memory Well through primary research.

If we want to set our story on the streets of inner-city Baltimore to create a show such as *The Wire* (2002), then nothing beats walking those streets. The stories, moments, locations, and characters will walk right past us. *The Wire* comes across as a very authentic show. It is still listed as one of the best TV shows of all time. The show's creator, David Simon, was formerly a police reporter in Baltimore.

He combined his personal experiences of covering stories about Baltimore with his writing partner's knowledge of working in the Baltimore Homicide Department. Simon must have worked hard generating all this primary research and it is evident in the series.

We too should begin to live our research. Even little things, such as a poster in a corner shop or a conversation overheard on the street, will add legitimacy and authenticity to the worlds we create when we write.

Harmony Korine spent the first few months of pre-production on the controversial *Gummo* (1997) shooting houses and people during his location scout in Nashville. What he discovered there, and the fact that he grew up in that community, adds to the authenticity of the film. He even used some of this primary research in the title sequence.

One of the best things about this on-the-ground research is that we are constantly activating all our senses. Later, when we write, we will consciously, or even unconsciously, tap into these senses. One can't buy that kind of research, and we certainly can't find it online or in a book.

MUSIC AND MEMORY

I've used the word resonance many times. As I indicated in chapter 1, "Resonance," one way the word is used is as a musical term. Music moves us in a singular way. There is a reason that most religious traditions integrate music in some form. Hymns, recitals, and chanting can stir us in a way that is often inexplicable and hard to articulate. Music speaks to us on a non-intellectual level: it appeals directly to our emotions, and easily gets stuck in our Memory Well.

Hearing a piece of music can help to trigger a memory. Every writer finds his or her own method of writing. As we saw earlier, Dickens wrote in absolute silence, but I sometimes write with music in the background.

One way to use music is to look through our scripts and find a "theme song" for each scene. Is there some piece of music that captures the feeling we want to achieve with the scene? Turn to the end of this chapter and do the Music Exploration exercise.

Now that you have found a piece of music that resonates with you and your ideas, can you imagine that specific song playing on the soundtrack? If so, why not play that piece as you write? It doesn't have to be the song that will finally appear in the movie and it isn't always good to mention the song in our scripts. It just needs to be one that inspires us to create emotional resonance with our scenes and images.

Some directors pump music while they shoot to get the actors and crew to feel the energy of the scene. We can do the same as we write. As Stanley Kubrick says: "A film is—or should be—more like music than like fiction. It should be a progression of moods and feelings."

Finally, music can help transport us deeper into our Memory Wells. If we are having trouble accessing the Memory Well, we can listen to some music from our past. How many times have you heard a piece of music and been instantly transported back in time? We can integrate music into our writing processes if we choose to. We may find that the right piece of music unlocks a flood of ideas and images that infuse our work with freshness and originality.

CHAPTER 5 EXERCISES

FIRST MEMORY EXERCISE

1. Try to recall your first childhood memory. What is the first thing you can remember? Don't stress about finding the right memory—just reflect back. It doesn't matter how early a memory it is, just bring one up.

2. Write down the memory. Flesh it out. What happened? Who were you with? What senses can you remember from that moment and how were they activated? What colors do you see?

3. Keep writing, but now go a bit deeper emotionally. What were you feeling at the time? What emotions do you associate with the event?

4. Once you have written it down, re-read it and meditate on it for a few moments. Spend some time sitting in the memory. Imagine how that scene would play out in a film. Can you picture it as an inspiring scene in a movie?

SADDEST MEMORY EXERCISE

1. Spend some time recalling your saddest memory. Sit with it, close your eyes if you want to. If you can't find the saddest memory, that's okay, just find a sad one. Place yourself in that moment and activate your senses. Write down some key words or phrases that remind you of this memory.

2. How did you express this sadness at the time? Did you express it? What actions did you take? Try and dig deep to recall as much detail as you can. Did you cry? Did you keep it in? Recall and write this down.

3. Once you are done writing, take a minute to re-read what you have written and meditate on it for a few moments. Spend some time sitting in the memory. And then think about how you could write it into a script.

ANGRIEST MEMORY EXERCISE

Don't get worked up doing this exercise. You need to be gentle with yourself. I don't want you to throw your laptop through the window in anger, but I do want you to briefly, quickly, and methodically access some of the times in your life when you were angry.

1. Spend some time scanning through your life, trying to identify your angriest memory. It doesn't have to be the angriest memory. Rather find any angry memory. Don't spend time comparing memories. Just choose one to access for now.
2. Now go back and recall what was happening. Where were you? Who was with you? What were the sounds, tastes, and other senses you experienced?
3. Now ask yourself the following important questions. What action did you take to express your anger? Was it physical? Was it verbal? Did you express it? Or did you hold it in? Imagine you were writing a line of action in a script. What line of action would describe how you expressed your anger? Try only writing what a camera can film or a microphone can record.
4. Pause for a moment.
5. Can you think of other moments in your life when you were angry? Scroll through your past from your youth up to the present day. You don't have to go in depth like you did in

step 2, just make a quick list. Write down what it was that was making you angry. Put this list aside for now. You will need it later in chapter 6, "Finding Your Theme."

6. Go back to the angriest memory you wrote down in step 1. Re-read it and meditate on it for a few moments. Think about how it would play out in a film. Can you imagine it in a movie?

7. Take a break. Take a walk. Shake it off.

HAPPIEST MEMORY EXERCISE

1. Scan through your life, as if fast-forwarding a movie, looking for the happy moments. See if you can identify the happiest moment of your life so far. Even if it's just a very happy moment, that's okay.

2. Write down where you were. Activate all the senses. Write down what images you saw. What sounds did you hear? What tastes were there? Was there a sense of touch associated with the moment?

3. How did you express your happiness? What physical actions or dialogue or other sounds did you use to express it?

4. Once you have written it down, re-read it and meditate on it for a few moments. Imagine how it would play out in a film.

MEMORY FROM TODAY EXERCISE

1. Think back on your day. Take your time. Don't fast-forward through it, go in slow-motion. Start with the moment that you woke up. Slowly page through your day. One moment at a time. Brushing your teeth. What did you eat for breakfast? Where did you go? Go through each moment of your

day like this. Does anything stand out? Is there a moment that was especially interesting? It could be as random as running out of cornflakes, your floss breaking, or something that happened on the bus to work. Anything at all.

2. Spend some time in that moment, even if it seems random, treat it with the same attention to detail that you did with the other memories. What were you doing? What were you feeling? What were you wearing? Who were you with? What were the sounds, sights, and other senses around you? Sit in that moment for a while.

3. Write down some details of that memory. Can you imagine how that moment would work in a movie?

MUSIC EXPLORATION

1. If you have a script you are working on, get it out or open it up on your computer. If you don't have a script, you can still do this exercise; all you need is a story idea.

2. Page through the script and find a scene that you really like. If you don't have a script, think in broad terms of a story you want to tell and hold that in your head.

3. Open up your music library on your computer or get out some old CDs. In other words, access your music.

4. Hold your scene or story idea in your head as you skip through your music library. Find a song that resonates with the scene.

5. Listen to the song a couple of times and see what ideas and images come up. Could these ideas enhance your story? Try and access your Imagination Well and your Memory Well during this exploration.

CHAPTER SIX

FINDING YOUR THEME

*"No tears for the writer, no tears for the reader. No surprise
for the writer, no surprise for the reader."*

— *Robert Frost*

When we embark on writing a screenplay, we are starting a journey into an ocean of infinite possibilities. It's easy to get lost. For many writers, it is the theme of our story that guides us. Theme should be a thread that runs through each moment and every sequence of our scripts. It links to a larger issue that the script explores. Every scene we write is an opportunity to communicate the theme to our audience. Our theme is like a compass, which makes sure that we don't get lost at sea.

Having said that, however, theme is a slippery term that is too easily bandied about by writing coaches and film critics. People will spend hours analyzing what a film's theme is and whether it was clearly communicated. The truth is, as a writer, I often don't know what my theme is until I've written three-quarters of the script. Sometimes it is clear only after the first draft. It's as if I have launched my boat into the sea, sailed around a bit, and then decided where I'm heading.

This is often the case with stories that "must be written." They are frequently so personal that the theme can elude us. We might flounder about for a while until a script editor tells us what it is that we are actually writing about. Once we have discovered our theme, even if it takes a few weeks, months, or even years, we may need to rewrite to focus it.

It might seem as if I am contradicting myself. On one hand, I say that theme is our compass, and on the other I say that theme is a slippery concept that we might find only halfway through our writing process. No one wants to rely on a slippery compass. It would be much easier for me to say that theme is something we need to discover before we write; that we should spend hours and days finding out what we want to say before we start writing.

For me, the truth is that to some extent theme falls into that category of mystical writing concepts. Like the word *resonance*, it is a difficult concept to nail down. It doesn't have the precision that writing instructors would like to think it does. It falls into elusive territory. Like the Muses and the Duende, theme is a tricky beast to grapple with. However, knowing our theme can empower us to be clear communicators.

The theme of our scripts should have something to do with the human experience. The deeper and truer the theme, the more our stories will resonate with a wider audience. The theme could be reduced to one word, for example, "greed" or "loyalty." It may be a statement, for example, "absolute power corrupts absolutely," "family is the most important thing in the world," or "we can overcome our addictions."

Our theme will start to answer questions like the following. What are we trying to say through our film? Which "issues" are we exploring? What argument or statement are we making about the world?

Luckily there are ways of using the wells to help us tune in to themes that interest us.

THEMES FROM THE EXTERNAL SOURCES WELL

When I look back at the movies I've made and the scripts I've written, I see common themes running through many of them. While this doesn't always happen, some writers often go back to the same issue over and over again. You may not be conscious of it, but if you look back over your work you too might find a few central issues repeated at the heart of it. These may even be related to what drives you to be a writer in the first place.

One way of finding out what themes matter to us is to pay attention to what moves us. As we have seen, almost any art form can resonate with us: books, plays, music, photos, opera, or movies. Since we are screenwriters, we're going to use other movies to help us find our themes. We could also redo the following exercise thinking of art forms beyond movies if we feel like it.

Turn to the end of this chapter and do the External Theme Exercise where you will be asked to look at movies that matter to you and extract a common theme from them.

In doing the exercise, did you dive into your External Sources Well and find movies that spoke to you? Did you discover any common themes at the heart of them? Remember, this list will change over time. Some films will replace other films. Depending on where you are in life, what interests you or what issues you are dealing with, your list will evolve accordingly.

When I do this exercise, the first thing I struggle with is finding the top ten films that I love. I watch lots of films and have taught and re-watched so many that the list feels like it could be endless. I have appreciated critically acclaimed movies like *Citizen Kane* (1941) and *Apocalypse Now* (1979) so many times that I can quote lines of dialogue with ease. However, these are not the types of films I would like us to use for this exercise. Rather than producing a critically acclaimed list, I would rather that we create a list that resonates with us personally.

My list includes the surfing movie *Big Wednesday* (1978). This is not because it is one of the best films of all time, it's because we had a VHS copy of it when I was growing up and I watched it over and over again. I think *Raging Bull* (1980) is in some ways a perfect film, but my list includes another Scorsese film, *Bringing Out the Dead* (1999). While objectively quite flawed, it spoke to me when I watched it at the turn of the millennium and struck something so deep inside me that I saw it three times in the cinema. The point is to choose films with your gut instinct.

Top 10 Films That Move Me:
The Shining (1980)
North by Northwest (1959)
Dr Strangelove or: How I Learned to Stop Worrying and Love the Bomb (1964)
Blue Velvet (1986)
Bringing Out the Dead (1999)
Dune (1984)
Cinema Paradiso (1988)
Big Wednesday (1978)
The Blues Brothers (1980)
The Godfather (1972)

It's a rather eclectic list. These are simply the films that resonated with me so much upon first viewing that I have watched them multiple times. I know that *Dune* is regarded by some, including its director, as a bad film. But I was thirteen when I saw it in the cinema and it had a profound effect on me. I even had the *Dune* action figures and used to pretend that I was the main character, Paul Atreides. It is not about the objective quality of the film, but whether it resonated with you.

There are a few themes I can see at work in my list. The first is "family—loss and restoration" which is evident in *The Godfather*, *Big Wednesday*, *The Blues Brothers*, and *Cinema Paradiso*. The second is "the chosen one" which is also in *The Godfather*, *Big Wednesday*, *Blues*

Brothers, and *Cinema Paradiso*, but also in *Dune*, *Bringing Out the Dead*, and *North by Northwest*. A third theme is "undercurrents of society" which I see in *Blue Velvet*, *The Shining*, and even *North by Northwest*.

This is not a precise science. I am sure I can find other themes and connections in the movies on my list. But through this exercise, I have used my External Sources Well to identify three themes: "family—loss and restoration," "the chosen one," and "undercurrents of society."

These themes are indeed found in a lot of my scripts. I hope that you found some themes to explore in your own films by visiting the External Sources Well in this manner.

THEMES FROM THE MEMORY WELL

Another way of finding our themes is more outside the box. We can access our Memory Well to discover which issues are important to us. In order to see what we are dealing with in our lives, let's take a look at what pisses us off.

Our anger is often sparked because of a perceived injustice done against the world or us. It might be a justified rage, or be a totally misdirected anger that actually points to something else we aren't yet aware of. From running workshops, and in my own writing, I have noticed that anger can be a very good marker as to which issues drive our stories and our need to tell them.

George Orwell said that, "when I sit down to write a book, I do not say to myself, 'I am going to produce a work of art.' I write it because there is some lie that I want to expose, some fact to which I want to draw attention, and my initial concern is to get a hearing." I'm not saying that we have to write a script to "get a hearing" to change something that angers us, but the energy around perceived injustices can be the source of healing stories.

So let's unpack our issues, starting with the word *issue*. One definition is "an important topic or problem for debate or discussion." A second definition, which I like, is "the action of flowing or coming out. The point of issue, an issue of blood." Our issues are often the place from where our desire to tell stories "issues" from.

So what are our issues? Let's get an idea by looking at what makes us angry.

At this point, turn to the end of the chapter and complete the Your Issues Exercise where you will recall and compare moments in your life where you have been angry.

It's important to realize that this process is a bit like peeling an onion. There are many layers. To illustrate this, let's go back to the angry memory I shared about littering and environmental destruction. Remember the red-faced kid lashing out at the billboard in the wetlands? The one the fishermen found so astonishing? Something that makes me angry as an adult is when people chuck cigarette butts out of their car windows. I can link when I was angry about the development on the wetland to when I become angry at seeing people litter. On the surface, they are both about a lack of respect for the environment. I am indeed moved by the issue of environmental degradation and have produced work around this theme.

But when I think back to the moment in the wetlands and dig deeper, another issue becomes clear. Before attacking the innocent billboard, I vividly remember the waterbirds walking around, looking for their nests. In retrospect, something else about that particular bit of my memory resonates with me. It speaks to me about missing homes. It could have been that I was missing something at my own home that day that made me angry. Perhaps that's why I was walking out to the wetlands on my own. It could be that I have an issue with family dynamics between parents and children.

That's another layer behind the anger. And that's exactly the theme I would like to explore in my next script.

This self-analysis will ideally develop and change as we grow and transform as writers and, more broadly, as human beings. The themes we may want to explore will change and grow as we change and grow. The idea is that if we are conscious of this process, it will help us write with more clarity and confidence. I don't mean that we have to write only from a place of anger. If anything, a lot of insight into the subtleties of writing from anger can be gleaned from this enigmatic quote from playwright Athol Fugard: "Love is the only energy I've ever used as a writer. I've never written out of anger, although anger has informed love."

Write down the themes and issues you have identified through this exercise. Set them aside. You can use them to inspire a new story. Or look back at an existing script and see if these themes are hidden somewhere in that story. Perhaps you haven't made them clear. Now that you can harness these personal issues, chances are that you will be able to focus your stories more clearly.

Having said all of the above, it is important to remember that we shouldn't make our issues the audience's problem. No one wants to watch a film that is full of our issues. That's not the point and is not what I am recommending here. There is a famous Samuel Goldwyn quote from when he headed up Metro-Goldwyn-Mayer Studios: "If you want to send a message, use Western Union."

There is a lot of truth in that quote and also a lot of cynicism. I agree with it in that I don't go to the cinema to tap into other writers' issues. I do, however, sometimes go to the cinema to learn about life. Even if it's a mindless film, I like to think that it could mean something. I'm looking for resonance. If you can add a theme or issue that I am concerned with, you are likely to have me hooked.

WRITING BIG THEMES INTO SMALL STORIES

Many of us want to address the big important themes like "death," "justice," "identity," or "love" in our writing. Sometimes we start writing inspired by these issues. We think, "I would like to write a script about loss and death." We might then invent a story about how a father's entire family is killed in an avalanche. We might imagine ourselves into the position of the grieving father in some morbid fantasy. The problem with this is that if we write from this position we are drawing from the Imagination Well only.

It might be that we are really interested in the injustice of suffering. And we might have even identified that from our Memory Well. But we have chosen to write about something that is foreign to us. These scripts often lack genuine emotion. The stories become insubstantial projections of what we think it would feel like to lose our family to an avalanche. If we are lucky, and masters of our craft, we might be able to get away with it, but more often than not, the movie we write may feel emotionally empty.

My question is this. If we want to write about the theme of death, why not write, for example, about the death of our grandfather instead? Write a story inspired by a small, intimate death experience.

When I am privileged enough to hear someone in one of my workshops share such an intimate moment, it always moves me. I'm not moved because the death is significant to the entire human race, but because it's significant to the participant, to the writer. Themes of loss, death, and injustice are clear when people share from the heart. They resonate.

When setting out to write and thinking about our themes, we should first take a look at our own lives and see where that theme has played out. Then, if we are writing a script from scratch, we should decide if writing a true story could be more powerful than an imagined one.

IT MUST BE WRITTEN

If we explore themes inspired by issues and memories from our lives, we may be able to discover the kinds of stories that must be written. If we are lucky, we will be visited by one of these golden-chick stories that just demands to be written. It might only be one story. One script. Perhaps we will write one fantastic script that gets picked up and made. Or maybe we have ten or twenty scripts inside us that must be written.

In the movie *Trumbo* (2015), we see a lovely moment that illustrates this. Dalton Trumbo, the great scriptwriter, has been clandestinely churning out movies for the studios and is asked if he has any ideas for something he really wants to write. Trumbo responds with, "A few. One keeps buzzing around up there, won't go away. Cleo and I were in Mexico at a bullfight, years ago. Bull died. A thousand people cheered. Three didn't. Cleo, me and a little boy down front. Crying. I always wondered why." Inspired by this memory, Trumbo then went on to write *The Brave One* (1956), which won the Academy Award for Best Story.

If you haven't yet been visited by a story that must be written, I hope that by doing some of the exercises at the end of this chapter you will start to discover those stories. The trick, I find, is to be open to them.

If we open the door to the things that matter to us, the stories "buzzing around up there" will find us.

CHAPTER 6 EXERCISES

EXTERNAL THEME EXERCISE

1. Take a moment and recall your favorite movies. This is not an objective best-movies-of-all-time list. Go for movies that you really liked, movies that intrigued you, films that have resonated with you in some way. They don't have to be critically acclaimed. They are the kinds of movies you have watched more than twice. Don't think about it too hard. List ten of them.

2. Look through the list and then step away from it for a moment. Take a short break. When you return to the list, check to see if there are any movies missing or some that could usurp others. In other words, see if any other movies have popped into your head that are more important to you than something already listed.

3. Now look through your list and identify the theme at the heart of each of the films. This exercise is about you so whatever theme you see in the film is the correct one. It might not be what the filmmaker intended or what academics discuss. The theme you identify is important.

4. See if you can group the films into distinctive sets that deal with similar themes. You might find that there is no clear connection between some of them. But you will likely find that there is a common thread connecting parts of your list together.

5. Now simply reflect on the themes that you have found. Do these themes resonate with you?

YOUR ISSUES EXERCISE

1. Turn back to your Angriest Memory Exercise at the end of chapter 5.

2. Take a look at all the angry moments you listed. Can you think of any more? Write down as many as you can.

3. Review your list. See if you can figure out what made you angry. What was at the heart of it? Next to each angry moment, briefly note what sparked it. Dig deep here. If your angriest memory has to do with road rage, for example, is there something else lying behind it? Is it perhaps less to do with bad drivers on the road but more to do with wanting to control the world around you?

4. Compare all the angry moments and the reasons you were angry. Are there any common themes? There are many different issues and things that make us angry, but is there a common thread in those you listed? Even if you only link two or three moments together, that is a great start.

CHAPTER SEVEN

A LIFE OF CHARACTERS

"Plot is no more than footprints left in the snow after your characters have run by on their way to incredible destinations."

— *Ray Bradbury*

The inspiration for our scripts might be a theme we want to explore, a personal memory of a life event, or it could be a character that we've seen or met. Movies that are written around a character often seem more authentic than movies written simply from an idea.

From my perspective, there is nothing more rewarding than finding two strong characters, putting them in a jar, shaking it up, and seeing what happens. As I write the script, the characters start developing on their own. Dialogue comes tumbling out of their mouths. If they start doing things that surprise me, even as I am writing them, then I know that they'll start writing the story for me.

FINDING CHARACTERS

Luckily for us, characters are everywhere. They are in the world as real people and can be found in fictional characters on the screen or in books. We can consciously use our wells to help us find and develop interesting characters.

We may want to draw from the External Sources Well to find characters. Many writers think of actors or characters from other movies and use their characteristics and identities to create a pastiche character. They might think of an actor like Jack Nicholson and imagine how a character would talk and behave, using Nicholson's mannerisms. Or they find a character like Rocky Balboa and channel his characteristics.

COLLIDING CHARACTERS

We can also take characters that resonate with us from our External Sources Well and collide them with each other, thereby activating our Imagination Well.

To experience this in action, turn to the end of this chapter and do the Colliding Characters Exercise.

Could you feel how you accessed your External Sources Well when you think of the characters from the movie and list them? Could you then feel how your Imagination Well was activated when you collided them together? We can discover some intriguing characters using this method.

Remember, there is no right or wrong way of doing these exercises. It is all about experiencing the wells and, with this exercise in particular, activating and digging our Imagination Well deeper.

It is not just new characters that are discovered when we collide characters. Like an atomic explosion, if we collide the right characters, our Imagination Well might explode with hundreds of ideas. We might discover plots, dialogue, and scenes simply by combining two characters.

If I combine the two characters used as an example in the exercise, Rocky and Princess Leia, I see a very interesting, strong, female boxer. My mind also starts to imagine a story of a real princess, say one of the British royals, who takes up boxing. My Imagination Well is activated and the next thing I know I have an outline for a story about Princess Kate getting into underground boxing and sneaking out of the palace at night to fight in disguise.

Then my imagination, influenced by the External Sources Well again, will picture a disapproving Queen who is controlling. If she finds out about the fights, then it's all over. Of course, she arrives at the climax of the movie, determined to put a stop to the title fight, but when she sees how athletic and talented her daughter-in-law is, she ends up cheering her on.

That's the way the Imagination Well works. Once we tap into it, the stories shoot out. Sometimes the stories aren't the most original, but they are there for us to tinker with.

If we are lucky, we access the Imagination Well and discover a completely new and unique character. Harry Potter came to J. K. Rowling in a flash while she was on a delayed train. These imagined characters can be very exciting to write, but if we don't root them in our reality by drawing from our Memory Wells too, they can come across as one-dimensional.

So, just as with themes and events, the problem with writing from the External Sources and Imagination wells, in terms of creating characters, is that it can often lead to imitation (just another Nicholson-type character) or pure fantasy (characters not rooted in the real world). J. K. Rowling's characters are strong because they feel as if they are linked to her personal reality. Hermione, Snape, Harry, and Ron's whole family seem to contain elements from Rowling's Memory Well. They seem to be drawn from the Imagination Well, but inspired by her life.

If we have discovered a character in our Imagination Well, it might be useful to collide them with characters from our Memory Well. Those characters have a head start because our memories are rooted in reality.

CHARACTERS FROM THE MEMORY WELL

The next exercise is going to require you to tap into your Memory Well. Notice how it still takes a moment or two to do this. Observe what this feels like. Become aware that the process of accessing our Memory Wells is often functionally different to what comes easily to us as writers.

Turn to the end of this chapter and do the Characters from Life Exercise where you will recall someone you have seen over the last few days that has stuck in your mind for some reason.

Did you discover an interesting character? The point of this exercise is not to create a character to center a script around, but if that has happened, fantastic. The point is to illustrate that we come into contact with interesting characters all the time. We just have to remember to remember them.

Two days ago, I was working at a coffee shop. At the table next to me was a family of three: a father, mother, and their son. The son was in his early twenties. He had a large frame. Close-cropped hair. Wearing a rugby shirt. But there was something else about him that caught my attention. His shoulders were slumped. His chest was slightly caved in. He looked like he was trying to diminish himself.

Then I overheard this fantastic line of dialogue. "Don't laugh when I tell you I want to be a vegetarian," he said to his father. And his father replied, "I wasn't laughing," and the guy responded, "I saw the way you looked at mother." To which the father said, "You're imagining it."

I was struck by how this big guy who looked so sure of himself, and seemed to take up so much space in the world, wanted to be a vegetarian and his parents were belittling him for it. This was an authentic moment revealing the complexities of life. He's a sports jock who wants to be a vegetarian. Here is a character. We have contradictions. We have complexity. It was all playing out right in front of me. Narrative fruit, ripe for the picking.

And this exercise only looks at the last few days. Imagine what a lifetime of encountering characters does for our writing. We have a massive resource we can draw from. We should make sure that we use it.

We can also collide characteristics of individual people from our Memory Well to create brand-new characters. Or we can take one tiny mannerism from someone that we know and create a whole character around that. Or give that mannerism to a newly invented character. We can mix and match names, characteristics, traits, occupations, and anything we find in our Memory Well with things discovered in our External Sources Well or invented in our Imagination Well.

I know a playwright who had a friend who always used to shush people. She would hold out her hands in front of her as if she were patting a large dog. Then she would push them up and down and say, "Shhhh, shhhh, shhh." It was a let's-not-disturb-the-status-quo gesture. The playwright took this quirk and designed a whole character around it. Each time the other characters would start talking about a complex emotional subject, this character would repeat the sound and gesture. By transferring this one mannerism, the playwright created a truly compelling character that was so neurotic and anxious about upsetting the apple cart that she never grew.

The point is that an audience will sometimes relate more with characters from life that have struck us for some reason, than with characters that we invent out of thin air.

POPULATE YOUR SCRIPT

As we become more aware of characters in our wells we may want to look through our old scripts and populate them with these personas, or use some of their unique traits and mannerisms. Even if our main characters have already been established and developed, we can still insert minor roles and populate our stories with quirky, dynamic, and distinctive people drawn from our wells. All the characters in our scripts should be memorable and different in some way. We could use our Imagination Well to do this, but I would encourage us to also draw from our Memory Well.

Turn to the end of this chapter and do the Minor Character Exercise where you will look through your script, if you have one, and identify your minor characters. Then you will look through your life, find interesting people, and try to mix and match them with characters in your script.

In one of my scripts, I wrote the part of a record store clerk. He was a pretty bland character. So I went through characters from my life, like flipping through an old-school Rolodex, and came across this guy who was a DJ at a goth nightclub. He is tall and thin with long black hair, covered in tattoos and piercings. His demeanor is very feminine. I was inspired, so I "copied and pasted" him as that character. I collided his character from my Memory Well with the character I had invented from my Imagination Well. It fit perfectly.

At the time, in the script, one of my main characters was a young single mom who was trying to sell CDs of her music to the record store. In one scene, she is rummaging around in her bag for the CDs and doesn't know what to do with her baby, who she is holding in her other arm, so she asks the record store clerk to hold her. The image of this goth holding a baby in front of his face as if it were toxic waste became really funny in my head. And then his next line, "It's against company policy," which referred to accepting the CDs, had a double meaning. Company policy didn't permit employee baby-holding either.

The point is to show that we have access to fascinating people all the time and that sometimes it works to pop them into our stories. We can, of course, use the spirit of this exercise and apply it to our main characters as well. Especially when we are fleshing them out and making them more three-dimensional.

DIALOGUE FROM THE MEMORY WELL

One of the most pleasing things that happens when my workshop participants write from their Memory Wells is that their dialogue becomes more dynamic. A lot of screenwriting is craft-based. The more we write, the better we become at plotting and character-ization. But writing dialogue is different. Some people are just great at it from the get go and others, like me, struggle with it. On average, about five percent of my workshop participants have a natural affinity for writing dialogue. The rest often end up writing clunky dialogue that might move the story forward, but doesn't seem genuine.

But no matter how good or bad their dialogue writing is, as soon as I ask them to tap into their Memory Wells, their dialogue starts to sing and ring true. Why is this?

The main reason is that we often approach dialogue writing with an objective in mind. We want to communicate specific informa-tion to the audience or we want the characters to communicate information to one another. In life, though, how often do we directly communicate with one another? Often we don't say exactly what we mean. Sometimes our words are stunted and unclear and we can't articulate exactly what we want or need from the other person.

Sure, there are some characters that are strong and straightforward, and if we have a character like that, we should write them that way. They can say exactly what they mean. But, for the most part, our job as writers is to hide the communication of information by writing casual, true-to-life dialogue. We still need to successfully get across whatever narrative information we need to in a scene, but through genuine-sounding dialogue. Not an easy task.

One of the reasons we enjoy watching films is because we get to unpack this kind of subtext. A lot of this meaty dialogue writing is happening now on some TV shows. Shows that are character studies, such as *Breaking Bad* (2008), where writers have more time to play the subtext, will allow for long scenes full of dialogue that doesn't seem to move the show forward, but which reveal a lot about the characters.

We can recreate dialogue like this if we tap into our Memory Well. Turn to the end of this chapter and do the Dialogue from Life Exercise. You will be asked to remember a moment in your own life where you had to communicate something important. The exercise will help you see how much was probably communicated in the subtext.

I am not suggesting that we fill our scripts with lines of banter about arbitrary things, or with characters not saying what they mean. Real-life speech doesn't make for fantastic screen dialogue, but at least it rings true. It might be worth going back to our scripts and seeing if any dialogue is too direct. We could access our Memory Well and recall conversations we have had. Does the dialogue in our scripts ring true? If not, we should change it.

Having said that, remember that the point of dialogue in screenwriting is to communicate something to the audience. We need to maintain a balance. We have to let the audience know what our characters want and how they feel about one another. We don't have much time to do it in. As much as hearing on-the-nose dialogue can be frustrating, it's also inefficient to write a script where characters only talk around the subject so they don't offend each other.

In a feature film, we generally have one or two moments when our main characters can say precisely what they mean. They can even express exactly what they want. More often than not, it's only once. Be on the lookout for that moment in a film. There is a great example of this in *The Godfather* (1972). Michael Corleone, the Don's son, meets with the leader of another mafia family, who was responsible for a hit on his father. Michael is ostensibly there to meet about a truce between the families, but plans to kill the mafia leader.

Michael clearly states his goal. The writers, Mario Puzo and Francis Ford Coppola, have Michael switch from speaking in Italian to English to draw attention to the importance of the moment. Michael wants to make sure that the corrupt cop at the table with them understands him, and the director wants to make sure the audience pays attention.

Michael assertively states, between gritted teeth, "What I want . . . what's most important to me, is that I have a guarantee. No more attempts on my father's life." He doesn't get what he wants and so, without giving it away, he decides to do something about it. The inner needs and desires of the main character have been clearly articulated for all to hear. This moment works. It lets the audience know exactly what the main character wants and the directness of the dialogue is motivated by the character's emotional state.

As this example shows, sometimes it's possible, and even necessary, that characters speak from the heart, with no subtext at all.

To get them to that point though takes a lot of preparation and a particular scenario. In *The Godfather: Part II* (1974), Kay, Michael's wife, tells him exactly how she feels about him when she says, "At this moment I feel no love for you at all. I never thought that could happen but it has." She doesn't mince words and lets him have it, but it's taken the writers one whole feature film and more than half of another one to get the character to the point where she clearly speaks her mind.

Again, we should look deeply into our own Memory Wells and see when we were able to say exactly what we felt. What were the circumstances that prompted it? What motivated us? Was it a particular person whom we usually communicate with this way? If so, as we write a script, we need to be sure that similar circumstances are in place before our characters candidly speak their true emotions, needs, or goals.

Another powerful way of tapping into the Memory Well when it comes to dialogue is to simply listen to the world around us. We should keep an ear open for dialogue. It's happening all around us all the time. Some time ago I overheard someone saying, "You can't make chicken soup without a chicken." I'd never heard that saying before. I'm still not certain of its deeper meaning, but I like it so much that it might end up in one of my scripts someday.

Even though we spend our lives swimming in a sea of dialogue, sometimes we don't listen to it. We are so used to the sea that many of us have tuned out the dialogue that is happening all around us. I find it useful to think of dialogue in musical terms. Just like a composer works with timbre, pitch, rhythm, and volume, so too can a screenwriter. We can listen to the symphony of dialogue playing around us each day, let it fill our Memory Well, and then re-create it in our scripts.

CHAPTER 7 EXERCISES

COLLIDING CHARACTERS EXERCISE

1. Think of some characters from movies that really resonate with you. It may be that the characters resonated while the movie didn't. Write the characters' names down, or a short description if you can't remember their name. List about ten characters.

2. Combine or collide the characters with one another. If, for example, one of your characters is Rocky Balboa and another is Princess Leia from *Star Wars*, try to imagine what character you could create if you combine them. You can combine any aspects of their characters. Character traits, emotions, and physical description. Anything. It is not a precise science. Have fun with it.

CHARACTERS FROM LIFE EXERCISE

1. Take a moment to think back over the last two days. Are there any interesting people that you met or saw? They can be anyone from a person you know very well to a checkout person at the store to a stranger on the street. Go methodically back through the last couple of days looking for a character. Choose someone that was interesting to you.

2. Spend some time remembering that character. What were they wearing? Did they have any unique mannerisms? Why did they stick in your mind? At this point, consciously continue to tap into your Memory Well only. Keep the recollections as real as you can. What sights, sounds, and colors did you associate with that person? Did they say anything memorable? Was there any dialogue you remember? If so, write it down.

3. Now that you have your character, consciously start tapping into your Imagination Well. Feel how different that feels. Imagine a short back-story for that character.

4. Take a moment to step away from the exercise and then re-look at the character you have remembered. Have you seen a character like that in a film before, or have you found an authentically new character?

MINOR CHARACTERS EXERCISE

1. Look through your script, if you have one, and identify minor characters who you don't think are that important. Maybe they only have one or two lines of dialogue, or maybe they have no dialogue at all. If you don't have a script, just imagine a scene in your head that takes place between a main character and this kind of minor character. Write down who that minor character would be. They could be the receptionists, checkout people, store clerks, etc., that facilitate the routine business of your script. List a few of these minor characters.

2. Think back on your life. Open your Memory Well and let attention-grabbing people in your life pop up. Don't try and control this process. Don't think of particular people. Just see who comes and then list a few people from your life. List between ten to twenty people.

3. You should now have two lists: the first is a list of the minor characters from your script, or imagined script if you don't have one, and the second is a list of people from your own life.

4. Now it's time to play. There is a children's game where you get a paper doll and all kinds of different clothes, shoes, hats, and other accessories that you can overlay to create

different characters. I want you to try that now with your minor characters. Go to the first character on your list, for example, "Receptionist 1" and then go to the list of people from your life and see if they fit into the role in your script. Some will fit. Some won't. They don't have to fit exactly; this is more of a free-flowing puzzle. Maybe only a couple of traits fit into the character in your script and not the whole person from your life. That is okay. Some of the combinations you choose might juxtapose too much and could be funny. For example, a cheerleader construction-site worker might just be too funny for the story you want to tell. Or it could be perfect. If any of them fits the tone of your story, why not adapt your minor character so that they inherit some of the traits of these people from your Memory Well?

DIALOGUE FROM LIFE EXERCISE

1. Think back to a moment in your own life when you had to communicate something very significant.
2. Exactly what did you say? How did you say it? What tone of voice did you use? Write down the dialogue that you recall. Even if you can't remember it exactly, that's okay. Spend some time in the Memory Well. Slow down the moment and try to remember what happened beat for beat.
3. Look at what you have written. Can you see how much of the exchange went under the radar? Can you remember if you communicated non-verbally? How much was said with a glance or a nod? Or did you say exactly what you felt?

CHAPTER EIGHT

ACTING FOR WRITERS

*"Acting is a question of absorbing other people's personalities
and adding some of your own experience."*

— *Paul Newman*

At the start of this book, we looked at the concept of resonance. It's true that scenes and events in films move us, but the main source of emotional resonance is with the actor. The actor is the instrument through which the emotions of the story are conveyed. It might sound obvious, but that moment when an actor moves us is the moment when their performance resonates with us.

If you are lucky enough to have had a script produced, or to have had a professional read-through, you will have seen that magical moment when actors inhabit your characters. For writers, it's often a mixed blessing, filled with both excitement and dread. Will they be able to truly inhabit the characters we have written? Will their articulation of the lines be the same as we imagined? Will they understand their character motivations?

An actor has a very different process compared to that of a writer. I have done some acting in my time and, in my experience, actors have to do a deceptively simple thing. They have to just jump into their roles using whatever tools they have at their disposal. They have to become the characters we create. It's a fantastic and almost mysterious moment. It's a moment that we need to pay attention to. If the actor turns around and asks, "What's my motivation in this scene?" it may mean that we haven't got the character quite right yet. To avoid this, I always suggest to my workshop participants that, to some extent, they become actors while they write.

So, what do actors do exactly? I love this question. I believe that actors, at the heart of it, don't always know exactly what they are doing. Mostly, they perform from instinct. However, acting techniques have been developed over the years to help actors grapple with their peculiar craft.

I want to share five acting terms and techniques that are useful to the writer. Connecting these techniques to the Three Wells will show how we can use them to breath life into our characters.

SENSE MEMORY

After doing the Memory Well exercises, you will have noticed how if we really place ourselves in a specific memory, we can make it come alive by recalling or imagining the sights, smells, tastes, sounds, and touch of the moment.

Actors use a similar method to access their emotions. If an actor has to pretend to be sad, rather than indicating sadness with their facial expressions, they look back at their own lives and find a moment when, say, they were feeling really hopeless and sad. They can then activate the senses around that memory, recall them in the present, and then feel sad on cue.

My cousin, who was a child actress, used to recall a moment when her chickens drowned. She had a cage with chicks in it and one day there was a storm. Their coop flooded and the chicks couldn't escape and they drowned. She stood there with the smell of mud and fresh rain in her nostrils and saw this horrible sight of her beloved chicks.

It's a dramatic image and a dramatic moment. There are, I presume, many sensory inputs she can draw from in that moment to recall the emotions attached to it. The feeling of the cold air on her skin. The sight of the dead chicks. The sound of the rain on a tin roof. The taste of her tears, perhaps. The smell of the muddied water. She would identify one or more of these sensations and use the recollection to transport herself back into that moment to help her express sadness or loss as she performed.

As brave writers not afraid to tap into our Memory Wells, we can use a similar technique to access memory and emotion while we write. Let's say that my cousin is a writer and not an actress. Perhaps she has to write a scene where a character is watching an airplane coming in to land with her husband on board and the plane crashes. It's one of those moments that certain scripts call for. But, thankfully, most of us haven't experienced that kind of tragedy. To make the moment real for herself, she could imagine the scene with the chicks. She could then use her sense memory to transport her back to that moment, but also to inspire the scene.

The idea is to recall the sensations of that time and then write the scene. Perhaps she would make it a rainy scene. Perhaps there would be a muddy mess at the end of the crash. Perhaps the character would run past a row of emergency workers and end up falling down in the mud. Maybe there is a dead pet that she sees that had been thrown from the hold and it stands in for her dead husband.

Even if we are using our Imagination Well we can activate our senses to really place ourselves into the scenes we are creating. We may surprise ourselves by the images, dialogue, and events that come up when we tap into our Memory Well and activate our sense memory.

SUBSTITUTION

In the example in the previous section I have substituted the story about the chicks into the story about the aviation accident. Substitution is an acting term where an actor will take an emotion they have experienced or a person they know and place it into a scene they are playing.

If we haven't had such a traumatic experience as seeing our pet chicks drowned, we can still use our sense memory to create dramatic scenes. There is a very likely apocryphal story I once heard about Sean Penn. The story goes that when he wants to resonate with disgust he thinks of . . . wait for it . . . flat cola. So yes, those moments when we see Penn looking disgusted with someone, he's digging deep and thinking of flat cola to get there.

This may not be a true story, but I like what it illustrates. We don't have to have experienced trauma to write something traumatic. When we access our Memory Well, we can substitute events that have given us a similar feeling to the event we are writing about. What matters more than the event itself is the emotion it evokes in us. It can almost be more useful to find one small thing to use, like Penn's flat cola, rather than dredging up all our past traumas each time we write a character experiencing something traumatic. As long as we get deep into our sense memories, and feel those emotions, our writing will be stronger.

For example, an actor might need to find the depth to play a scene where their child is kidnapped. The actor might never have had someone they love be kidnapped, but they can look at the actor playing their child and substitute someone they love for the actor. Or they can even think of a moment when they lost something precious to them. Then the actor can amplify that memory to get into the emotion of the scene. To the viewer, the scene feels more real because the actor is tapping into true emotion they have felt.

When writers attending my workshops start tapping into their Memory Wells, some claim that they have lived very sheltered lives and that they don't think they have the life experience to write important stories. They feel their well is empty.

It's an understandable response. Many films depict fantastical events. We see a film, for example, about a daughter being kidnapped and a father killing half of the Russian mafia in an attempt to get her back. Or a film about a man blowing up an asteroid to save the Earth. We see movies about brothers killing brothers or friends hurting friends. Films often depict significant and extraordinary events. The first thing writers attending my workshops often ask themselves is: "How can my life events compete with those noteworthy events?"

Then, an amazing thing happens. They start sharing their memories with others and, even if the memory is as straightforward as their favorite dog dying, if they share it honestly, by the end of their story everyone is in tears.

It's not the magnitude of the event that matters, but rather the subjective experience of the person sharing it that gives it weight. If we can communicate that emotion through our scripts to the screen then we will find resonance with an audience.

So, our life experiences might not be as fantastical as those depicted on the screen. We may have to write about an event that is far removed from our lives. Perhaps, for example, we have to write about a soldier in World War I who is looking into the eyes of his dying comrade. If we have never seen someone die, how do we access a real memory that is required to write an authentic scene?

We could tap into our External Sources Well and be inspired by scenes from other movies. We could activate our Imagination Well and try to empathize with the characters and imagine ourselves in their shoes. Or we could ask ourselves: what emotions in our Memory Wells can be linked, even tangentially, to the soldier's story?

When I was a teenager we had a dog named Wrinkles. This dog and I had a special bond, but as I grew up and Wrinkles got older, we eventually had to put her down. I had just gotten my driver's license and my parents were away so I had to take her to the vet myself. I insisted on being with her until the end. I looked into her eyes as she died and I remember seeing the life drain out of her. Recalling it now, it seemed that some sort of film covered her eyes as she died. Her eyelids didn't close, her eyes just died as her head grew heavy in my hands.

If I were to write that soldier scene, I could tap into this memory. I might have the soldier hold his friend's face and look into his eyes as he is dying. Time could slow down. We could see a close-up of his buddy's eyes as the life drains out of him. His face gets heavy. Jowls hang down. Maybe just that one visual image is enough to trigger the emotion I felt as I watched my dog die.

The idea is not to directly compare our lives to the dramatic events we want to write about. The point is to discover authentic emotions in our Memory Wells and then translate that emotion into the stories that we are creating.

To try this in practice, turn to the end of the chapter and complete the Substitution Exercise. You will be asked to find a scene in your script, if you have one, and find a memory from your own life that can be substituted into that scene.

Drawing from the Memory Well and substitution can be so powerful that we can even take something we have felt and put it into a totally different situation and it will still ring true. Let's say, for example, my father left home when I was younger and that left me with a feeling of deep abandonment. If I can harness that memory, and that feeling, I can write with truth about a similar story set anywhere in the world.

I could write about a young boy living in a North African desert village who is in love with a village girl whose family is about to leave. I could take that feeling of abandonment and transplant it to the North African village. The script might still resonate with an audience. If I just wrote that story without tapping into my inner truth and life experience, it would almost certainly read as fantasy. I would be drawing from the Imagination Well only and the story could feel contrived. If I haven't done my research it may even be insulting to the society that I am writing about. But by tapping into my Memory Well and transplanting a personal truth, I may be able to write about almost any scenario and still let my special experience shine through.

THE MOMENT BEFORE AND AFTER THE SCENE

When writing a scene we writers have an agenda. Each scene is part of an overarching plot and contains a bit of information that we want to communicate to the audience. We know, for example, that for our protagonist to head off on a journey of self-discovery there has to be a motivating factor. For example, she gets fired from her job. So we have to write the firing scene for our plot to move forward. That is the narrative point of the scene. We start writing the scene knowing the outcome.

Crucially, however, the characters don't know the outcome of the scene they are in. They don't know they are about to be fired. Life happens at random and, as much as we would like to think otherwise, we don't know what's going to happen next. Actors too, having read the script, will know the outcome of the scene. But they have to be in the moment when they act, as if they are experiencing it for the first time. They have to "forget" the events in the script. To achieve this, some actors use the "moment before the scene" technique.

The moment before the scene is another acting technique that is useful for writers. It refers to an imagined moment in the world of the character. An actor, about to appear in the scene, will imagine what their character was doing just before the scene begins. In this way the actor carries the character's past into the scene with him or her.

It's the same for our characters. They should enter all scenes blind and carry their past with them. To achieve this, some actors will conduct a scene analysis that goes beyond what is written on the page. Let's unpack this a bit more in relation to writing using the Three Wells.

The moment before the scene is really a simple concept, but a lot of writers in my workshops misunderstand it at first. Let's look at it very closely. Imagine a movie that plays out exactly like this. Scene 1: Our main character wakes up in the morning. Scene 2: She arrives at her office. Scene 3: At lunchtime she enters her boss's office and is fired. On the page we have three scenes following directly on from one another.

But in a lived life the character would experience the time between the scenes. Clearly some time has passed between scenes 1, 2, and 3, but what happens during that time is not relevant for the narrative. To a person in the real world, though, what happens in the moment before they enter their boss's office affects their behavior. In other words what has happened between scenes 2 and 3, and particularly the moment just before scene 3, is important.

Actors will invent a moment before the scene so that when they appear in scene 3, they carry some emotion into the scene with them. For example, they may imagine that the main character had a very frustrating morning. Perhaps someone was parked in her parking spot. Then the coffee machine ran out of beans. Then her computer wouldn't connect. Note that the actor is making all of this up. It's not in the script.

When an actor carries these daily moments into the scene it generally makes their performance more present, alive, and layered because they are carrying an emotional memory into the scene with them.

Experienced actors instinctively use their Imagination Well for this kind of scene preparation. They might also access their Memory Well. Many of us have had a moment when we think we need caffeine and the coffee machine is empty, or when we are about to eat some cereal and the milk turns out to be sour. We can use little moments like these to put ourselves in our character's shoes.

We writers can also use our Imagination Wells or, more powerfully, our Memory Wells to invent a moment before the scene just before we write the actual scene. It gives the scene depth and adds to the subtext. It helps to make the audience feel that the character is living in the real world.

To illustrate how this works, turn to the end of this chapter and do the Moment Before the Scene Exercise where you will be asked to find a scene in your script and apply the moment before the scene to it.

It's very important to remember that the character doesn't have to directly refer to her frustrating morning in the scene. She doesn't have to mention it in dialogue or have a coffee stain on her shirt.

It's all in the subtext of the scene. No one has to see it necessarily or even know what happened in the moment before the scene, but it informs the emotional tone of the scene.

So, the next time we sit down to write, we could first spend some time thinking about what our characters were doing just before we cut to the scene. We could pause. Access our Imagination and Memory wells and put ourselves in our character's positions before the scene and then start writing. We may be surprised by what comes up.

Unlike when the actor does this, we might invent new dialogue and actions. It might even make us want to rewrite or add material to an existing script.

We should always be careful not to add too much material, as we always want to start a scene as late as possible. We don't want to spend a minute of the scene having our characters walk into the room, shake hands, say their hellos, and talk about their moment before the scene. We need to get into the meat of our scenes as soon as possible, while making sure that our characters carry the moments before the scenes with them.

We could find the time to apply this exercise to every scene that does not follow on directly from another one in our scripts. We might discover that we can add richness and depth if we bring the world beyond the scenes into all of our stories.

Since there is a moment before, there is also a moment after the scene. In life, we usually have an idea of where we are going to go when we leave a room. Again, an actor will create a story for their character and imagine where they're going as they exit a scene. If they are going to pick up their kids from school, they may walk away with purpose. If they have parked their car in a loading zone they may seem anxious and leave in a hurry. If they have to go back home from a coffee shop to write a script they are struggling with, they might seem strangely reluctant to leave.

We don't have to write the actual moment after the scene, but we should have an idea of what it is. Like the moment before the scene, the characters may reference it directly or it may just add to their energy and demeanor as they exit the scene.

Feel free to now take the Moment Before the Scene Exercise and do it as a Moment After the Scene Exercise.

Whatever you do, remember that these pre- and post-scene moments are not supposed to extend the scene. Just as it is best to enter the scene as late as possible, it is also best to leave as early as possible. We shouldn't waste time showing our characters saying goodbye and walking out of the room unless it is crucial to our story. We should leave as early as possible, but let our characters carry their imagined futures out of each scene.

If we surrender to our characters and let them experience the scene in the moment, as an actor does, and use our Three Wells in the process, we should create more layered and interesting story moments.

YOUR GOALS/NEEDS VS. THE CHARACTER'S GOALS/NEEDS

Another technique actors use to be in the moment is to have clear scene goals and needs for their characters. Even if an actor just has a simple goal, they can improvise a scene and be in the moment and make interesting discoveries. Goals can be small goals, such as "fire my employee," or they can be overarching goals (goals that stretch over a whole movie), such as, "I want to rule the world."

Most books about screenwriting incorporate this technique in some way and will ask us to explain what our character wants. This goal, then, drives the story forward. John Truby has done some excellent work around the concept of a "desire line," which he explains as the trajectory of the movie that forms itself around the character's desired goal. As we write a feature film, this "desire line" can keep us on track. Like the theme, it is a compass that directs the whole story. If we know what our main character wants and needs, it focuses our writing.

Many writers who attend my workshops struggle to define their main character's needs and goals. There is a reason for this. When writing stories that matter to us, stories that must be written, we often can't see what our main character's needs and goals are. This is because we are too close to the story. I witness this so often that I would be surprised if other writers don't also struggle with this.

When I sit down to write scripts inspired by my Memory Well, it's often easy to identify the supporting characters' goals and needs, but the lead character's goals, and especially his or her needs, are sometimes less obvious to me. This is because our personal needs can often be confused with our lead characters' needs.

Here is an example. There is one script that I have written various drafts of over a few years. I thought that the lead character's need was simply to leave suburbia. It was only much later in the process that I realized that his need was actually to stop being afraid. He was too scared to leave because suburbia was familiar and comfortable, even though he hated it there. Fear was holding him back. What I didn't realize at the time was that I had a similar fear and my character's journey was a reflection of my own. I couldn't identify his need until I understood that my own fears were also holding me back.

The challenge, then, when writing films that must be written, is that we have to look into our own lives to identify the themes and drives that we have and then we might see them mirrored in our main characters.

Of course, just like a main character in a film, we often can't clearly articulate our needs. Years in therapy might get us closer, but often our needs linger in shadows and we have to work hard to identify them.

While it may be hard for us to discover our main character's need, it's often crystal clear to people who read our scripts. That's because they don't have the attachment to our main character that we do. My workshop participants often present work and I see needs operating in the story that they are oblivious to. Going back to my own experience as a writer, it took partnering with another writer on my suburbia script for me to see what was really happening at the heart of the story.

If we are struggling to find a strong and clear need or goal for our lead characters, we could examine our own lives. This is by no means an easy task. It may be one of the most difficult things to ask. It means not just looking into our Memory Well to find cool scenes and stories, but to interrogate our own motivations, needs, drives, and desires.

If this type of reflection becomes part of our writing processes, it can be healing and transformative, not just for the audience, but for us as writers too. If we can develop a sensitivity and maturity that allows us to knowingly transfer some of our own struggles into a main character's trajectory, we are more likely to profoundly move an audience.

BECOMING THE CHARACTER

There are almost as many ways for an actor to get into character as there are actors. In my experience, each actor has their own system that works for them. Some will discover the character in their bodies by walking around until they find how their character walks. Others may use their voice, searching for their character's vocal pitch and speech patterns. And others might go shopping for shoes until they find the pair their character would wear; then they can literally step into their character's shoes. Some simply just act and be the character, with no conscious system at work.

All or none of these techniques might be useful to us writers, depending on who we are. Many writers wouldn't be caught dead walking up and down in front of their computers trying to move like their character, or shopping for their character's shoes. That's okay.

However, there is one exercise that most of my workshop participants find very useful. All it requires are two chairs, one for you and one for your character. Turn to the end of this chapter and do the Becoming the Character Experience. In this exercise you will use a character you know from your Memory Well.

We can do this exercise for all the characters we create. Of course, when we do it for characters that we have invented, we will activate our Imagination Wells more than our Memory Wells. You can repeat the Becoming the Character Experience using a completely fictional character that you made up in your script to feel this process in operation.

Once you have completed the exercise you may want to make notes about what you have discovered about the character. Note down physical aspects but also, importantly, emotional ones. What did you feel for the character when you saw them? When you sat on the character's chair and became them, what did your character feel about you?

As with most of the exercises in this book, the emotion and the resonance we feel while doing them is more important than anything else. We have to be open to feeling things and then expressing them in our writing.

Becoming the character worked very well for Bruce Robinson when he wrote the British cult classic *Withnail and I* (1987). Robinson is an actor and writer. He has said that, "Acting, writing, direction—I see them all as aspects of the same thing. Essentially I'm a dramatist, and I act it out when I write." As well as becoming his characters as he wrote, the characters and story of *Withnail and I* came from Robinson's Memory Well. The character of Withnail was based on a friend and the whole tone of the film is drawn from a time of his life when Robinson was, as he puts it, "a chronic alcoholic and resting actor, living in squalor."

The authenticity of this film and its fresh approach and tone is a direct result of Robinson drawing from his Memory Well. The fantastic dialogue and interesting scenes are probably a result of Robinson becoming his characters as he wrote.

CHAPTER 8 EXERCISES

SUBSTITUTION EXERCISE

1. If you have a script already, find a scene that is a low point or a high point in the narrative. If you don't have a script, think of a scene in a movie that is a high or low point in the narrative.

2. Access your Memory Well and see if you can substitute a moment from your own life where you were feeling something similar to the emotions in the scene you chose. You may have to heighten the emotion that you felt in your memory to make it fit the scene. Can you relate to what your character is going through if you use your Memory Well moment? Can you get closer to what your character would be feeling in the scene?

3. Reflecting on the previous steps, are there any images, moments, or senses that you can take from your Memory Well and add to your scene to make it stronger?

MOMENT BEFORE THE SCENE EXERCISE

1. If you have a script, get that ready. If you don't have a script yet, that's okay. Just like in the previous exercise, you can use a scene from any movie.

2. Look through your script and find a simple scene between two characters. It can't be a scene that continues directly from the scene before it, there must be some time before the scene begins that is not in the script. If you don't have a script, just choose a moment between two characters in any location. You don't have to write it down.

3. Imagine a moment before the scene. Choose one of your characters. What happened to them just prior to being in this scene? Try and draw from your Memory Well and imagine a scene from your own life, big or small. The event doesn't have to be significant or dramatic, but it should be a moment that has an emotion attached to it. Make it something real, authentic, and believable to your story world.

4. Do the same thing for the other character. Remember, the moment before the scene applies to each character individually. Unless they were with each other beforehand, they will have experienced different moments before the scene.

5. Now, revisit your scene. Consider the perspective of your characters, remembering the moment they now carry into the scene. Does that emotion shift things in the scene? Do you want to change any dialogue? Are there any actions or physical descriptions that should be changed? If so, do it!

BECOMING THE CHARACTER EXPERIENCE

1. Get two chairs and make them face each other.

2. Sit in one chair. Relax and close your eyes.

3. When you open your eyes imagine the character from your Character from Life Exercise sitting in front of you on the opposite chair. With your eyes open, imagine that you can see them sitting here.

4. At first, try and recall all the details you can about this person from your Memory Well. Have a look at their characteristics. What do they look like? How do they hold themselves in their body? What are they wearing? Take in as much as you can.

5. After a while, or perhaps even very soon, you will start to activate your Imagination Well. That's great. Try and fill in more and more information about this character as you see them in front of you.

6. Stay staring at them for at least three minutes. Things will come to you. Notice how you feel about your character. Are you threatened, attracted, intimidated?

7. When you feel like it, cross over to the character's chair and sit in it. Become the character from your Memory Well. Sit as they sit, feel some of their emotions. Look at the chair where you were sitting and imagine how your character would feel about you, the writer, sitting there.

8. Then sit back in the chair you started in. Close your eyes. Relax.

9. Write down any discoveries that you made.

CHAPTER NINE

A SENSE OF PLACE

"Look at the places where no one looks at, so you can see the things no one sees."

— *Mehmet Murat Ildan*

There are many reasons why locations are important. Choosing where to set a scene is one of the primary things we writers have to do. To really understand our characters, we should understand their surroundings. As Winifred Gallagher writes in her book, *The Power of Place*, "Modern science is confirming that our actions, thoughts, and feelings are indeed shaped not just by our genes and neurochemistry, history and relationships, but also by our surroundings."

She then goes on to show that our immediate surroundings affect our lives a lot more that we may think. There is received historical knowledge that the spaces around us are important. Feng Shui and other fields of study, as well as oral tradition and simple common sense, show us that our environment affects us directly. It's important to remember that our characters are affected as much by their surroundings as by their relationships or events in their past.

A good screenwriter will be able to transport the reader, and finally the audience, into the locations that they create. In this chapter we will look at how to use the Three Wells to enrich our films with specific locations that have resonance, as well as how to transport ourselves to imagined locations and experience them as our characters would.

LOCATION, LOCATION, LOCATION

One of the simplest ways of injecting originality into our scenes is to set them in original locations. Think about the example used earlier in the Graveyard Exercises. As we write, our minds often first go to clichéd graveyards and it takes some effort to redirect them to our Imagination and Memory wells. From there, we can access fresh ideas for graveyard locations.

Sometimes we create predictable locations because we write with plot at the forefront of our minds. For example, we may know that, at a certain point in our story, our main character has to break up with his girlfriend. For the plot to move forward, we have to write a breakup scene. So when we sit down to write the scene we are starting with a plot point in mind. If we start from that position, as in the graveyard scene, our minds might go to the External Sources Well first. Just like we have experienced with the Graveyard Exercise, the many breakup scenes in our External Sources Well have colonized our minds. So where would we set our breakup scene?

What was the first thing that popped into your mind? Remember, the first place we usually go to for ideas is the External Sources Well. If that's the case for us, we might have pictured a bedroom, dining room, or kitchen. This could be because we often think of breakups as domestic affairs and so these fights are often staged in the home. If we write from plot first, there is nothing wrong with setting the breakup scene in a bedroom. It will serve the plot. We can tick off "breakup scene" from our beat sheet and move on. But the question is, is this true to our lives, and is it unexpected or different?

If we draw from the Imagination Well, we can imagine a breakup taking place anywhere. Writers, aware of the cliché of the domestic breakup scene, often set these scenes in imagined spaces, such as restaurants, which offer the opportunity for public humiliation or embarrassment. But even this has become clichéd. It might be more cinematic to use the Imagination Well to set a breakup scene at an airport departure lounge, or on the rim of the Grand Canyon.

As usual with the Imagination Well, though, we must be careful. We should be wary of getting too carried away and set our scenes in strange locations just for the sake of it. Remember that we are after originality, but also believability and resonance.

When inventing a location for our breakup scene, we should also, of course, access our Memory Well. The best way to do that is to do the exercises in this book so that we learn to feel ourselves accessing our memories. Turn to the back of this chapter and do the Location Exercise.

After doing the exercise, some of you might have written bedroom, kitchen, or dining room because that is your truth. That is okay. This is not a competition to see who has had the most dramatic breakups in the most spectacular locations. If you did break up in a bedroom, could you transport yourself back to that space using your senses? If you did, can you recall any specific thing about that bedroom that then makes it a unique location? For example, can you recall a poster on the wall, a view out the window, a sound, or anything that makes the space unique? If you want to, then even though the location is a bedroom, you can still make that bedroom distinctive.

Drawing from my own experience, one breakup moment springs to mind. It took place in a nightclub. I was about nineteen and out with my girlfriend and other friends. We broke up on the dance floor. I remember having to go to the bathroom and standing in the small toilet stall, walls all painted pitch black. I could hear loud music pumping through the walls. I remember the dead-weight feelings of a teenage breakup with some self-indulgence thrown in as a song by Joy Division called "Atmosphere" played in the background.

So, through that exercise, I found a toilet stall in a nightclub as a location. Remember that all the wells share the same ground water. They all bleed into one another. To be honest, the breakup might not have played out exactly as I remember. It might not have been Joy Division playing in the background.

This illustrates how the Imagination Well affects the Memory Well. We imagine certain things from our past when we recollect. As long as our imagination doesn't taint our memory too much, that's okay. It's tapping into the emotion of the event that is powerful, not being specific about the when and where and whom. The point is that I now have a location, a toilet stall in a nightclub. I can now set any scene there.

Let's move away from the breakup scene. We can set any scene in any location, as long as it makes sense for the plot and characters. If you have already written a script, I encourage you to go through every scene and ask yourself if the scene is set in the right location? Does the location speak to the theme of your story? Is the setting cinematic?

Now turn to the end of this chapter and do the Random Location Exercise. You will be asked to recall locations from your own life and mix and match them with locations in your script, if you have one.

Once you have identified your location, you can flesh it out by using your senses. Turn to the end of this chapter and do the Location Using Senses Exercise. You will go back to the Location Exercise and activate both your Imagination and Memory wells.

Did you manage to successfully transport yourself back into your location using your senses? Did you activate it and embellish it using your Imagination Well?

If we can transport ourselves back to a specific place and time, we should be able to successfully transport a reader into our locations in our scripts. Once we have felt what it is like to be in our locations, we will have to communicate that feeling to the production team through our script.

EXPERIENCING LOCATIONS FROM THE IMAGINATION WELL

Very often, however, the locations we place in our scripts might well be made up. Whether we are drawing from life, or purely using our Imagination Well, the next exercise will illustrate how to place ourselves in invented locations and experience them as vividly as we have experienced locations from our Memory Well.

Turn to the end of this chapter and do the Painting Locations Experience. It requires not only a pen and paper, but for you to get up off your seat and use your body, imagination, and memory.

Did you get to imagine yourself in the location?

That might have felt like a strange exercise. It works at two levels. We just drew from our Imagination Well to create a space, but if we really focused, we will know, to some extent, what it feels like to live in that space. For a moment, we will be able to access our character's lived experience and create a memory of that space ourselves. For a moment, we have stepped into our character's Memory Well!

During my workshops, at this stage in the process, many participants make tiny but vital discoveries for their stories. You might have found a prop that your character uses or you might really get in touch with your character's emotional state. Did your character like the space they were in? Did they want to leave it? Did they feel comfortable?

Take a look back at the scene in your script, if you have one, that takes place in the location you used for the Painting Locations Experience. Have you captured some of the emotions, senses, and essence of the location in your descriptions? Are there one or two sentences you could add or rewrite that will better capture what you felt in the room?

My workshop participants who actively engage with this exercise are often richly rewarded beyond just discovering physical descriptions of their locations. One, for example, who was struggling to find her main character's goal, sat in her character's bedroom and felt an urgent need to get out of there. She, the writer, felt her character's drive, which was to get out of the small town she grew up in. It proved an invaluable insight for her. It wasn't directly related to the location, in that she didn't go back and rewrite the scene description, but it focused the drive of her entire narrative.

COMMUNICATING SENSES
EXPERIENCED IN LOCATIONS

One major constraint with scriptwriting is, of course, that we mostly write only what the camera can see or the microphone can pick up. If I were writing a novel, I could describe all the senses I imagine in a location and the reader would experience them. We are more limited with screenwriting. Without using voice-over, how do we indicate the smells or tastes that our character experiences? There have been some brief attempts by cinemas to tap into the sense of smell, for example, by releasing odors during films, but these gimmicks such as Smell-O-Vision and Scent-O-Rama never took off.

The movie *Perfume: The Story of a Murderer* (2006), set in 18th-century France, is a great example of how the filmmakers used visuals to activate the sense of smell. The film's plot is driven by this sense because the main character is a perfumer. In one scene, where the main character arrives in a big city for the first time, the filmmakers evoke the sense of smell by filling the location with barely perceptible smoke as he walks through the crowded streets. We see various images, each evoking a specific smell, including two wealthy women in a carriage, one hugging a small dog. There is a slow-motion shot of a horse breathing out of its nostrils. One of the women cools herself with a fan. We can imagine a waft of perfume.

Other shots follow: elegant people pouring wine, eating oysters, powdering their wigs, and smoke coming from someone's foul-looking mouth. The sense activation continues as we see textiles, flowers, tumeric, seeds, coffee, freshly baked bread, snails, cheese, coal, someone examining their rotting gums in a mirror, a child's feet in a muddy puddle, and freshly inked manuscripts.

This film really focuses on the sense of smell and ours might not, but the point is that we can use images to activate the audience's sense of smell, through activating their own memories of smells. We could use a similar technique when activating all the other senses.

Going back to my breakup scene, if I were writing the scene in the nightclub toilet stall I would have descriptions like: "Hand on wooden toilet stall door, stains of urine on the floor, loud music and voices."

I am not suggesting that we spend a lot of our precious script space writing out long descriptions about what our locations smell, feel, taste, sound, or look like. Many of the people in my workshops do this in great detail and there is nothing that screams amateur more than long bits of action describing a location. That is prose writing. We should always remember that screenwriting is more like writing a telegram: short, precise, and to the point.

The trick is to distill the senses down into one or two specific and descriptive props, actions, or sounds that we can express in one or two sentences—like the smoking, the warm bread, and the clip-clop of horses in *Perfume.*

And finally, a word of warning. Even though locations can make or break a movie, and even though writing a series of interesting scenes set in captivating locations may result in an interesting movie, remember that our plots must add up to something. Otherwise our audiences will be let down by just watching a series of excellent scenes that go nowhere.

It is essential to hang those fascinating scenes onto a solid structure. We may use the exercises in this book to strengthen our scenes, but we must always make sure that there is still a narrative thrust at the heart of our stories.

This book is intended to help us draw from our unique wells of creativity to make our ideas stronger. It focuses on being innovative in the moment of creativity. It doesn't focus on structure. Be sure to take a look at some of the books on plot in the Suggested Reading section.

CHAPTER 9 EXERCISES

LOCATION EXERCISE

1. Take a moment to look back through your life and recall any breakups that you have experienced. Think back through all the people you have been romantically involved with and try to remember the exact moment when you called it quits. If you haven't broken up with someone, you can use a story of a breakup a friend or family member might have told you about. I know that it might be painful, but look back and see what you remember of the moment.

2. Write down where you were when the breakup happened. What was the location?

RANDOM LOCATION EXERCISE

1. If you have already written a script, get that ready. If you don't have a full script yet, that's okay.

2. Look through your script and list a few of your locations. Do this at random. Don't choose the most interesting locations; just flip through, look at your slug lines and write down a few. If you don't have a script, pick a few scenes from your favorite film.

3. Now go into your Memory Well and think back on your life. Try to see what locations pop up. Don't try and control this process. You might find anything from the school cafeteria to a clothing store to a friend's backyard. They don't have to be particularly interesting places. Like with the Minor Characters Exercise at the end of chapter 7, make a list of some places that you have been to that for whatever reason have stuck in your mind. List about twenty of them.

4. Now you should have two lists. One is a list of some loca-
    tions from your script and the other is a list of the random
    locations from your life.
5. Do a similar thing that you did with the Minor Characters
    Exercise. Take the locations from your script and mix and
    match them with the locations you recalled from life. Does
    setting them in this new location add anything to the scene?
    Does it make it more cinematic? Does it add a layer of
    humor or danger to the scene? Does the scene now speak
    more clearly to your theme?

LOCATION USING SENSES EXERCISE

1. Think back to your breakup memory. If you don't have one,
    think of another powerful moment from your past. Really
    imagine yourself back in that moment. Spend some time
    sitting in that location. Answer the following questions. It is
    okay to use your Imagination Well a bit more during this
    exercise. Make sure you write down your answers, even if
    just in bullet point form:
    - What did the location look like? What colors were
      present? What shapes?
    - Do you associate any smells with the location?
    - What did it sound like there? What noises did you hear?
    - Are there any tastes you associate with the moment or
      location?
    - What about the sense of touch? Do you remember what
      anything felt like to the touch?

PAINTING LOCATIONS EXPERIENCE

1. Choose a location from your script. If you don't have a script, picture a location from a movie you have seen. Start with an interior location for now. Later, you can do this for an exterior location, but interior ones are easier to start with.

2. Get up and move to the center of the room you are in right now. Ideally you do this experience in your bedroom. If you are reading this book on the train or other public space, save this exercise for when you are back home. Close your eyes and picture yourself in the location from your script.

3. Imagine that you are in a white space. A bit like a virtual reality room with nothing projected onto it yet. Start drawing on that space. Physically indicate drawing on it. Use your hands as if they are paintbrushes. Start with the large objects: a door over here, a window there, a book-shelf there, or a bed here. Use big brush strokes. Don't get into the details yet. If you are drawing a window, just draw a rectangle for now. Don't force things into the room that wouldn't naturally be there. The space is three-dimensional so you can turn around and draw behind you, too.

4. Once you have drawn all the main objects, move in closer and draw some details on each one. For example, if you have drawn a bed you could add some pattern to the pillowcase. If you have drawn a bookshelf you could fill in some detail, names of books or colors of covers. If you have drawn a window you may want to draw the blind or the curtain.

5. When you feel like it is finished, sit down in the center of your room. Imagine what you have created around you.

Activate your senses and access your Imagination Well. What does the room look like? Where is the light in the room coming from? Is there any? What does it sound like? Are there any sounds coming from outside? What do the floor or walls feel like? What does the room smell like?

6. Feel what it feels like to be in that room. If you created the room from a script you've written, imagine what your character feels like when they are there.

7. Now bring in even more details. Get up and walk to where you drew the window. If you didn't then, draw one now. Look out the window. What do you see? Draw that. Spend a moment there. What do you feel when you look at that view?

8. Step away from the window and back into the room. Imagine yourself as the character that occupies that space. Ask yourself, as the character, "What do I want?"—in the room, in the scene, in the film.

9. Finally, take one last look around the room. Look for something you haven't seen before. Perhaps there is a part of the room that you didn't spend much time creating. Look there now. What do you see?

10. Take ten minutes and write about this experience and what you discovered about the location and your character.

CHAPTER TEN

LIVE LIFE

"How vain is it to sit down to write when you have not stood up to live."

— *Henry D. Thoreau*

f you have applied the techniques in this book and done the exercises, you should have:

1. A better understanding of how resonance works in films;
2. Experienced drawing from the External Sources Well, the Imagination Well and the Memory Well;
3. Seen that all the wells are connected;
4. Learnt how to consciously dig your wells deeper;
5. Discovered themes and issues that are important to you;
6. Learnt how to find and develop characters; and
7. Reimagined your locations.

Take a minute to look back on that journey. You have come a long way.

This final chapter will be a call for us to go out and dig our Three Wells deeper going forward. But before we do that, a few more suggestions about strengthening the Memory Well: some inspiration, some warnings, and some calls to action.

HITTING THE RIGHT TONE

As we know, when we watch a movie, it enters our External Sources Well. We remember certain scenes, settings, lines of dialogue, and music. We might recollect elements of the plot and if we are story-focused writers, we might even recall most of it.

However, I don't believe anyone can remember every moment of a film. Perhaps a savant, but even that is unlikely. Having edited feature-length documentaries, I can confidently say that even the editor, who is very close to the final film, can't hold the whole thing in their head. A lot of it, for sure, but not every single shot of every single scene.

What we remember of a film, and what becomes lodged strongly in our minds, is the overall tone of the film.

I love the word *tone*. To me it links strongly to the word *resonance*. Tone has many meanings but I am going to focus on this one: "a modulation of the voice expressing a particular feeling or mood." For our movies to resonate with audiences in the way that we want them to, we need to pay attention to tone.

Another way to think about this is that a film enters our External Sources Well through the plot, but the experience of watching the film goes into our Memory Well, and that is largely through the film's overall tone. It's the tone and the emotional resonance of a film that the audience holds onto when they leave the theater.

Remember that when we tap into our Memory Wells we are not recalling specific events, but emotions surrounding an event. Our Memory Wells hold past experiences, regardless of what details we remember. It's the same with a film. We leave the cinema with a new emotional experience that is now lodged into our Memory Well. We might leave the cinema with an overall happy tone resonating with us. There are as many tones as there are emotions. Films may, for example, have a sad tone, an upbeat tone, a quirky tone, an eerie tone, a nostalgic tone, or an adrenaline-infused tone.

Ultimately, it's the production team—and not the writer—who create the final tone of the film. We write the script and then others, in bringing it alive, express the tone. Tone is articulated in production design, special effects, lighting, cinematography, sound effects, music, and all the elements that come together to create a film. So how do we, as writers, make sure we communicate the right tone?

The only way a screenwriter can truly affect a film's final tone is through the strength of the words on the page.

A film or TV show is a product and it's assembled like a product on a production line. A script goes in one end, it is developed and worked on, and a movie comes out the other end. If you are lucky enough to get your script into production, you will witness this process firsthand. If we have a script with bad instructions, we'll find that the production team may misunderstand it and the film will not come out with the tone we intended.

Many talented industry professionals will read your script looking for specific words, signs, and indicators that tell them what to do. A scriptwriter is like an architect who has drawn a plan for a building and given it to a construction crew to build. If we don't clearly communicate what we want the team to do, they will do whatever they want. For example, if we leave out a character description, the casting director will cast whomever they want, rather than someone who fits the character that resonated with us from our wells.

This does not mean that we should include exactly whom we want to cast or specific camera directions, shot sizes, or copious amounts of production design detail in our scripts. The making of a film, after all, is a collective creative process. Our task is to inspire the team to communicate our tone. Their job is to take our vision and make it even better. If we get that right, we will feel comfortable enough to sit back and let the team run with our ideas, knowing that the correct tone will be struck at the end of the process.

This is part of the craft of screenwriting and may take years to get right. The trick is to read scripts to get a sense of how other writers do it and to write and rewrite our own. Ernest Hemingway said that the six golden rules of writing are, "read, read, read and write, write, write."

When I ask my workshop participants how many of them have read, say, ten feature film scripts, more often than not, none of them can raise their hands. It seems that we think that because we have watched many films, we are automatically qualified to write them. This is irrational. It's like thinking that just because we like music, we can automatically write a score for an orchestra. Or that because we have seen and been in many buildings that we can draw up a plan for a skyscraper!

First-time screenwriters, and even accomplished ones, should, of course, read scripts. That way we can see how the writers have managed to incorporate that illusive tone into their work.

Jill Soloway captures some of the cheeky tone of *Transparent* (2014) in her pilot script with lines like the following, describing the suburb of Silverlake in LA: "Hipsters wait in line for expensive coffee, lock up fixed-gear bikes, subconsciously compare beards." Of course, we won't see the hipsters literally comparing their beards, but the tone of her writing captures the tone of her series.

The Walking Dead (2010) has a totally different tone. The stylish horror of the original graphic novel is captured in Frank Darabont's writing like in the scene when main character Rick discovers corpses in the dark: "Match goes out. Pitch black. Rick breathing. Wondering if he should risk another match. Is he near the lower landing? He can't take it any more. We hear the matchbook. He lights his next-to-last match." The writer is breaking old-school screenwriting rules by writing what the character is thinking, but it captures the tone of the moment.

This kind of writing may take years to craft, but if we start off consciously knowing that our aim is to communicate emotions experienced in the Three Wells via the tone of the film, we will have a head start.

I'VE GOT TO TELL YOU THIS STORY

I find it interesting that people at my workshops often claim that they struggle to find good stories to tell and yet, as the workshop begins, I sometimes have to shout above them chattering to get their attention. There is something charged in the air before the workshop begins. What are they talking about?

Remember high school, when something had happened to you, or someone had told you something and you were just dying to tell that story to someone else? You get to class, find your friend, and you're about to launch into the tale and then the lesson starts. You sit through the whole class with this story burning inside of you. Or perhaps you arrive at work and want to tell your colleague about something that's happened but you are called into a meeting before you get the chance to do so.

That charged state of "I've got to tell you this story" is something alive and electric. Those stories. That feeling. Those moments in our Memory Wells, and the order in which the events are told when we retell them, have something I like to call "narrative currency." It's alive, like an electric current. It's valuable. We should be able to sell stories like that because, if we want to tell them so badly in the real world, someone may want to pay to see them on the screen.

When we come across stories like these in our Memory Well we should pause. We should take a look at them. What is it that gives them this narrative currency? What is working on a plot level? We will probably find that the story has some kind of twist, some kind of reversal. There will be surprise and intrigue. There might be stakes that are raised. There might be a lesson that is learnt. Or lessons not learnt.

All of the things that make a beautiful, enticing, and dramatic plot are contained in those stories that we just have to share.

We shouldn't discount them. These charged stories are in our Memory Well for a reason and they are all around us all the time. They are worth more than we can imagine.

WHAT HAVE I WRITTEN?

As we near the end, let's briefly reflect again on the process of writing. As I outlined in the Preface, this book was written by a writer for writers. It focuses on the act of writing. As such, I used myself as a case study and shared some of what I have experienced in the process of writing this book.

The idea for this book came to me organically. I have been exploring these concepts for the last twenty years as a workshop facilitator and writer. I didn't have a clear idea of how the concepts would be organized when I started writing. Very often when we write from the gut, or grapple with the stories that must be written, we don't know what will materialize. If we have a script that must be written, we might write it on spec despite the fact that we don't know what it is or how it will end.

In the past, when running workshops where writers want to write a script quickly, I asked the participants to write a logline first, then to work their way up to a scene outline and then write the first draft of the script. Many screenwriting books and courses work this way, starting with structure first. This system works and it may save us time and make the mammoth task of writing a feature film more manageable.

Having said this, allow me to play devil's advocate. The kinds of stories I would love to see come to life are the fragile ones. Echoing the Nick Cave quote from the Preface, I hope that we will discover stories in the bottom of our wells that are fragile and nuanced. These are stories that don't easily fit into loglines. They are challenging, subtle, and we have to treat them with care. We should be open to these stories. We should seek them out within ourselves and look for them in the world around us. We can play in our Imagination Well or spend some slow time in the Memory Well and then write a rough draft from the heart.

Writing is rewriting. The rewrites and edits of this book took much longer than the vomit draft. We will rewrite our scripts many, many times. But we might only be able to see the form of our scripts once we have completed a first draft. When starting to write we might think that our idea is a feature film but it could turn out to be a TV series. Perhaps it ends up working better as a short film or a stage play. We need to remain open to the fact that our finished product might not end up being what we set out to write. We have to honestly recognize what we have created once we have created it. And to do this we have to take a step back from it.

So when we sit down to edit our work, we have to step into the position of a trusted audience member and ask ourselves, "What have I written?" Then, once we clearly know what it is, we must make sure to retain that form as we rewrite. We should be brave. We should be ruthless.

This book is an example in point. The first couple of drafts were more a rambling of ideas. The more I wrote, and rewrote and rewrote, the more I focused on the idea of the Three Wells. The book, like a live thing, began to shift and change its shape until it settled into the text before you.

I can already feel the screenwriting training fraternity fuming at the suggestion that we should write organically and then discover our stories as we write. We could waste years of our lives doing that only to discover the story we are writing doesn't work. Of course, this kind of organic writing isn't the correct process for everything we write. If we are doing something on commission or writing to a deadline, then we don't have the time to find our stories organically.

As with most of the suggestions in this book, we have to find a middle ground as we integrate these techniques practically in our writing lives. I am not trying to turn us into starving artists toiling away at a block of marble. But I do want to give us the freedom and fortitude to nurture the stories that really matter to us.

IT'S THE END AND YOU KNOW IT

One of the final things my workshop participants struggle with is finding the perfect way to end their films. Endings are difficult for even the best filmmakers. There's the famous story of Francis Ford Coppola stressing about how to end his film while in the middle of the jungle during the shooting of *Apocalypse Now*. So how do we know when "it is written"?

Earlier, I mentioned the idea of the tabula rasa. The painter looks at a blank canvas and picks up a brush with an idea in mind. The carver looks at the block of marble with some idea of what they want to find inside. They add more and more layers of paint, or chip away at the marble, until they come closer to revealing the artwork they had in their heads. A true artist knows when to stop. As Michelangelo puts it, "I saw the angel in the marble and carved until I set him free." How did he know when he was finished carving and that the angel was ready to fly?

How do artists know when that magical moment is? Many would probably say that they "just know." It is intuitive. Just like these artists, the screenwriter needs to know how to end a script and I have to know when and how to finish this book.

Even now, as I write this, the ending somehow eludes me. The same can be true of a script. There is one thing that can help us know when to end our stories that I would like to share. It is contained in one of the most important questions a screenwriter can ask himself or herself: What do I want my audience to feel when they leave the cinema?

If our theme is the compass keeping us on the right path, then what we want the audience to feel when they leave the cinema is our destination. If we have tapped into the Three Wells and found a theme that we want to resonate with our audience, then it is very important for that theme to ring out clearly right at the end. That buzz the audience is on when they leave the cinema is them resonating to the tone of the film and, ideally, to the tone of our wells. We need to be clear on what that final resonance is.

What do we want the audience to feel from our stories? Elation? Adrenalin rush? Sadness? Remorse? Conflicted? Sometimes they will feel multiple things. The answer to this question will inform every scene that we write and especially how we end our film.

If we struggle to find the right ending for our scripts, we can revisit our wells, rediscover our themes, and then figure out how we can communicate that to the audience in the final moments.